THE
ORIGINAL
REVOLUTION

Essays on Christian Pacifism

By
John H. Yoder

HERALD PRESS, SCOTTDALE, PENNSYLVANIA

Christian Peace Shelf Series

The Christian Peace Shelf is a series of books and pamphlets devoted to the promotion of Christian peace principles and their applications. The editor, appointed by the Mennonite Central Committee Peace Section, and an editorial board, from the Brethren in Christ Church, General Conference Mennonite Church, Mennonite Brethren Church, and Mennonite Church, represent the historic concern for peace within these brotherhoods.

1. *Nevertheless* by John H. Yoder. 1971.
2. *Coals of Fire* by Elizabeth Hershberger Bauman. 1954.
3. *The Original Revolution* by John H. Yoder. 1972.

All Scripture citations unless otherwise indicated are from *The New English Bible,* © The Delegates of the Oxford University Press and the Syndics of the Cambridge University Press, 1961, 1970. Used by permission.

THE ORIGINAL REVOLUTION
Copyright © 1971 by Herald Press, Scottdale, Pa. 15683
Library of Congress Catalog Card Number: 76-181577
International Standard Book Number: 0-8361-1572-4
Printed in the United States

THE
ORIGINAL
REVOLUTION

In this book of essays on Christian pacifism the author seeks to restate in various moods and modes the conviction that the renunciation of the sword to which Jesus called His disciples is one of the keys to the rest of the problem of Christian faithfulness and to the recovery of the evangelical and ecumenical integrity of the church. Ideas are presented in both expository and argumentative styles.

The content is divided into two sections under the headings, Biblical Perspectives and Ecumenical Perspectives. Chapter titles are: The Original Revolution, The Political Axioms of the Sermon on the Mount, If Christ Is Truly Lord, If Abraham Is Our Father, Let the Church Be the Church, Christ the Light of the World, and Christ the Hope of the World.

The author has written to the Christian who has become aware of the problem of war and of the inadequate moral guidance that has been given by the churches in the past. A book for anyone interested in answers to the problem.

To
Bishop Carlos Gatinoni

At whose invitation the title essay
in this collection was first delivered
as a sermon in the
Iglesia Metodista Central of Buenos Aires

PREFACE

In the late sixties an enormous proliferation of interest and imagery around the concern of Christians for social change became evident. A new book dealing with "the revolution in theology" or "theology for the revolution," with politicking as a theological concern or with theology as a political event appeared almost every week.

Despite some overlapping both in language and in substance, the present publication is not to be understood as arising out of or catering to the faddist approach to theology which most of this rhetoric represents. Some of the material included here was first written well before this fad arose, and it is being prepared for publication in the relaxed confidence that by the time the book can reach the market its title will no longer be in style.

There is a growing awareness in churches and seminaries that the problem of war is at the heart of much of the sickness of modern society, and a growing recognition that the traditional Christian approaches to this problem, namely the just war and the crusade, are becoming increasingly inadequate as sources of moral guidance and are beginning to look as if they never were adequate. Yet there exists no contemporary accessible compendium of thinking about how a pacifist commitment can fit within the wider axioms and commitments of Christian thought.

There was a time when Christian pacifists published very significant symposia, much of the substance of which would even today be worthy of continued respectful attention; [1] but the latest of these lies ten years back. There has been no dearth of treatments of the thought of certain heroic figures (Gandhi, King), but often such treatments only increase the reader's doubt about whether the position the great man took can live without him. There have been a few personal statements, most of them at least a decade away.

Denominational statements have come from the so-called "peace churches," but not recently, and such statements can hardly avoid being pigeonholed as being less relevant beyond their borders. [2] Finally, we do have a definite recent history [3] to add to the (less thorough) surveys of earlier experience, [4] but these do not seek a coherent contemporary synthesis.

It is thus more under the vacuum of a particular need than under the pressure of any conviction of personal apostolate that I have accepted the invitation to gather a body of essays which seek to restate in various moods and modes the conviction that the renunciation of the sword to which Jesus called His disciples is one of the keys to the rest of the problem of Christian faithfulness and to the recovery of the evangelical and ecumenical integrity of the church in the age of the atom.

The essays differ. Sometimes the style is expository and sometimes argumentative. Sometimes the reasoning process is finely woven and sometimes impressionistic.

Sometimes the position taken may seem closely allied to tradition and sometimes unprecedented. Sometimes the assumptions it makes about the Bible, history, or the church will seem intolerably naive, [5] and sometimes unjustifiably cynical. The author is aware, as the reader soon will be, of the spottiness in style which results. That no effort has been made to recast all the text in the same mold is justified, if at all, by the conviction that the unity of fundamental commitment to Christ and His cross, foolish to those who seek wisdom and weak to those who seek strength, but to those who believe, the wisdom and power of God may come through all the more clearly in, with, and under this diversity.

Footnotes

1. Percy Hartill, ed., *Into the Way of Peace*, James Clark, 1941; Percy Hartill, ed., *On Earth Peace*, James Clark, 1944; Harrop Freeman, ed., *Peace Is the Victory*, Fellowship Publications, 1944; John Ferguson, ed., *Studies in Christian Social Commitment*, Independent Press, 1954; Rufus M. Jones, ed., *The Church, the Gospel, and War*, Harper, 1948. Following that came a row of studies by individual theologians. The most substantial individual work is that of Jean Lasserre, *War and the Gospel*, Herald Press, 1962. Of the same order but less thorough are Charles E. Raven, *The Theological Basis of Christian Pacifism*, Fellowship, 1951; Culbert Rutenber, *The Dagger and the Cross*, Fellowship, 1950; and Edgar Orr, *Christian Pacifism*, C. W. Daniel Co., 1957.

2. The most substantial restatement in the Historic Peace Church context has been the work of the Mennonite Guy F. Hershberger, *War, Peace, and Nonresistance*, Herald Press, 1953, and *The Way of the Cross in Human Relations*, Herald Press, 1958.

3. Peter Brock, *Pacifism in the United States from the Colonial Era to the First World War*, Princeton University Press, 1968.

4. Roland H. Bainton, *Christian Attitudes Toward War and Peace*, Abingdon, 1960; Geoffrey Nuttall, *Christian Pacifism in History*, Blackwell, 1958, reprinted by World Without War Council, Berkeley, 1971.

5. A more responsible encounter with the scholarly disciplines of New Testament studies is offered in the related publication, *The Politics of Jesus*, Eerdmans, 1972.

CONTENTS

BIBLICAL PERSPECTIVES

I. THE ORIGINAL REVOLUTION*

1. The Old Words and the New Agenda

"So wonderfully has he dealt with me,
    the Lord, the Mighty One.
    His name is Holy;
his mercy sure from generation to generation
    toward those who fear him;
the deeds his own right arm has done
    disclose his might:
the arrogant of heart and mind he has put to rout,
he has brought down monarchs from their thrones,
    but the humble have been lifted high.
The hungry he has satisfied with good things,
    the rich sent empty away."   — Lk. 1:49-53

In the whole body of Jewish and Christian liturgy,
only a very few texts might be more widely known —
and more vainly repeated — than the two songs from

---

*Rewritten from a sermon last preached at the Eisenhower Memorial
Chapel, Pennsylvania State University, November 24, 1968.

the beginning of Luke's Gospel.

One of these songs is found on the lips of the maiden Mary. Catholic tradition knows it by its opening word *Magnificat,* "My soul doth magnify the Lord." But what it says is the language, not of sweet maidens, but of Maccabees: it speaks of dethroning the mighty and exalting the lowly, of filling the hungry and sending the rich away empty. Mary's praise to God is a revolutionary battle cry.

That simple observation should suffice to locate our topic. The fad word in the last few years of both Protestant and Catholic social thought is "revolution." From the black ghettos of the U.S. to the 1968 World Council of Churches Assembly in Uppsala, from the archbishop's residence in Recife to the Ivy League seminaries of the American Protestant establishment, from Peking to the Sorbonne, the slogans are the same. The system is rotten. Those whom it oppresses should submit to its tyranny no longer. It deserves nothing other than to collapse in upon itself, a collapse we will engineer.

It would be worthwhile sometime to dwell at more length on the way in which the term "revolution" confirms the intellectual relevance of Gresham's law, according to which the coinage with the least substance, value, and character will get the most circulation. The word "revolution" has passed through so many hands, over so many tongues and pens, that most of its meaning has worn off. Shaving cream is revolutionary if they put lime perfume in the can with the soap. The compulsory village relocation program in the Mekong delta was rebaptized "Revolutionary Development" after the 1966 Honolulu conference. But the fact that a

14

word can be prostituted or violated does not take its real meaning off our serious agenda.

The old word, the technical term, for the change Mary was rejoicing in is "gospel"; but "gospel" has become a tired old word. For some, it means the invitation to an individual to accept the forgiveness of sins, so that to preach the gospel, to "evangelize" is to spread the message of this invitation. For others, it means correct teaching about the work of Christ, so that "evangelicals" are those who hold to traditional doctrines. Elsewhere "evangelical" simply is the current word for "Protestant." For still others "gospel" represents a particular kind of country music.

If we are ever to rescue God's good news from all the justifiable but secondary meanings it has taken on, perhaps the best way to do it is to say that the root meaning of the term *euangelion* would today best be translated "revolution." Originally it is not a religious or a personal term at all, but a secular one: "good news." But *euangelion* is not just any welcome piece of information, it is news which impinges upon the fate of the community. "Good news" is the report brought by a runner to a Greek city, that a distant battle has been won, preserving their freedom; or that a son has been born to the king, assuring a generation of political stability. "Gospel" is good news having seriously to do with the people's welfare. Today we might speak of the end of the Vietnam war, as good news in this sense; not merely an event that makes some of us happy, but one which shapes our common lives for the better.

This is not only true of the meaning of the word we

15

translate "gospel," in its ordinary secular usage outside the New Testament; it is true as well of the story
which the New Testament calls by this name. Mary's
outburst of social enthusiasm in the *Magnificat* is only
one sample; but the response of her kinsman Zechariah
to the birth of his son is to sing that God has now come

> " . . . age after age he proclaimed
>   by the lips of his holy prophets,
> that he would deliver us from our enemies,
>   out of the hands of all who hate us. . . ."
>
> — Luke 3:9-11

When this son John began his own preaching, Luke
describes as "evangelising the people" his predictions:

> "Already the axe is laid to the roots of the trees,
>   and every tree that fails to produce good fruit
>   is cut down and thrown on the fire."

To those who asked him "What shall we do?" he answered:

> "The man with two shirts
>   must share with him who has none,
> and anyone who has food
>   must do the same."

Once again; whatever it is that God is about to do, it
will be good news for the poor, bad news for the proud
and the rich; it will be *change*, including changed economic and social relations.

  This was the expectation that Jesus Himself picked
up, when in terms almost identical to John's, He an-
nounced that the "kingdom of Heaven is near" and
then more precisely:

> "The spirit of the Lord is upon me
>   because he has anointed me;

he has sent me to announce good news to the poor,
to proclaim release for prisoners
    and recovery of sight for the blind;
to let the broken victims go free,
to proclaim the year of the Lord's favour."

— Luke 4:18, 19

The year of the Lord's favor or His "acceptable year" is the Jubilee, the periodic economic leveling-off provided for by the Mosaic law. Such a change is what Jesus says is now coming into view in His beginning ministry. It will involve attitudes, so it can be called "repentance," *metanoia*, "turning-the-mind-around." But it also involves social practices, "fruits worthy of repentance," new ways of using possessions and power. The promised coming change involves social and personal dimensions *inseparably,* with none of our modern speculative tendency to dodge the direct claim on us by debating whether the chicken or the egg comes first.

This was John's agenda, and Jesus'; but it is also ours. Between their time and ours, there have been other ages when men were more concerned with other questions, other priority agenda. There were centuries when men were especially aware of the fragility of life and its brevity; they wanted a word from God that would speak to their fear of death and the hereafter. Man's basic need was seen as his mortality. In this context it is no surprise that Christian preaching and poetry dealt with mortality and that the good news man needed was spoken in terms of eternal life.

In other societies, other cultures, men are plagued by anxiety, guilt, fear of judgment. In this context the good news is stated in terms of forgiveness, acceptance by God, and acceptance by other men. Today some rephrase it as self-acceptance. In still other ages, other cultures, man thinks of his need as primarily for help in getting a job or in facing sickness or poverty. To this as well the Christian message can speak. Men are still asking these questions, and Christian preachers are still proclaiming good news in all these ways; why should they not?

But for Jesus in His time, and for increasing numbers of us in our time, the basic human problem is seen in less individualistic terms. The priority agenda for Jesus, and for many of us, is not mortality or anxiety, but unrighteousness, injustice. The need is not for consolation or acceptance but for a new order in which men may live together in love. In His time, therefore, as in ours, the question of revolution, *the judgment of God upon the present order and the imminent promise of another one,* is the language in which the gospel must speak. What most men *mean* by "revolution," the *answer* they want, is not the gospel; but the gospel if it be authentic must so speak as to answer the *question* of revolution. This Jesus did. He accepted the phrasings John had made current; He proclaimed the coming kingdom and let Himself be called (though reticently, and subject to misunderstandings and redefinitions) the Anointed One *(Messiah),* or the Awaited One.

2. The Four Ways

Time has not changed as much as some think. In any situation of social conflict and oppression there are a limited number of possible strategies. Born a displaced person in a country under foreign occupation and puppet governments, Jesus faced the same logical options faced in 1778 by a Pennsylvanian, or in 1958 by an Algerian, or today by a Vietnamese or a Guatemalan. As He set about being the expected Messiah and representing in the world the cause which He called a kingdom, the situation surrounding Him, the men whose expectations He spoke to, and the tempter who accompanied Him through His career all joined to ask of Him a particular kind of behavior to reach His goals. He had four choices.

One way to begin, which was open to Jesus as it is today, was that of realism; to begin by accepting the situation as it really was. The Romans were in control of Palestine (much more solidly than the French in Algeria in 1958 or the Americans in Santo Domingo in 1968); any hope for change must begin with that reality. A brand new start is not an available option; we must save what we can by aiming at what is possible. This was in Jesus' age the strategy of the Herodians and the Sadducees. These were not, as a superficial reading of the Gospel narrative might make one think, nasty and scheming people; they were intelligent leaders following a responsible strategy. Their concern was to do the best one could in the situation.

Their rationale was simple and honest; one could not change the fact of Roman rule whether one desired to do so or not. "Let us then save what we can by aiming at what is possible." These were the people who were able to keep the temple worship going, to maintain the public recognition and teaching of the Jewish law. They preserved a breathing space for the Jewish people and culture; a unique, legally guaranteed status for the practice of a non-Roman, monotheist religion. It will not do to condemn them all unheard any more than it is honest today to condemn some people unheard as "establishment." They were working for justice and for change, and not at all without effect. Their work included some very costly — and effective — nonviolent direct action against the desecration of their temple by the Roman armies. But of course, in order to change it, they accepted and directly sanctioned the social system of Roman occupation under which they lived, and from which they profited. Yet this was in the interest of doing the best one could with the options available, only biding the time till more sweeping change could be engineered.

This stance is still very much alive today. For some, it is taken in an uncritical, pro-establishment way. Despite the theoretical separation of church and state, our society is never without a chaplain in the army, in the congress, and in the Memorial Day parade. It is the service of the chaplain to sanctify the existing order with the hope of being able progressively to improve it. A powerful publicity organization bears the name, "Religion in American Life." These are the people who advertise that by the use of religion "you can lift your life." What the religion is does not matter too much. It is assumed that it can be Protestant, Catholic, or Jewish; and if it were Buddhist or Muslim that would not change the point very much. This is likewise the concept which is at work when the interpreters of politics tell us, quite independently of any particular moral choices he might make, that President Eisenhower, or

Kennedy, or Johnson, or Nixon can be called "a very religious person."

But a similar stance is taken as well by many who are more critical. Much of the noisy social criticism of our day comes from "established" agencies; from the staff of councils of churches or of mainstream denominations. Criticism of American military policy in Vietnam, or of investment policy in South America or South Africa, has in the late 1960s often come from the tenured faculty of the endowed Ivy League universities and seminaries, trying to turn America's "good guy" self-image in upon itself as a judgment instead of a justification.

But for Jesus, the strategy of "infiltrating the establishment" was not a temptation at all. Of the four available options, it was the only one which never could have come to His mind. This party was against Him from the beginning; in fact, from the time of His birth. It was their head, Caiaphas, who stated that it was expedient that one life should be sacrificed — whether justly or unjustly mattered little — for the sake of the community.

For it does come to this; if religion is to sanction the order that exists it must defend that order even against criticism of the prophetic word, even at the cost of the life or the liberty of a prophet. The critic-from-within-the-establishment, the house prophet, will, if he stays inside when the crunch comes, be with Herod after all. This has not changed in our day.

The clearest alternative to the establishment path was that of righteous revolutionary violence. It was presented in Jesus' time by the underground political and military group called the Zealots, men in the heritage of Joshua and the Maccabees, for whom the "zeal of the Lord" was to express itself in holy warfare against the infidel Romans. The Romans understood no other language than that of force; no other means can be effective than a response to them in their own kind. Zealot revolutions rocked Palestine about once a generation in the decades before and after Jesus.

Today as well the Zealot temptation is beckoning. In Christian student organizations, both Catholic and Protestant, and in the 1966 conference on Christian Responsibility in Modern Society in Geneva, voices are loud which proclaim that the only option for the Christian church is to "take sides" with those forces which demand immediate social remodeling, even at the cost if necessary of much bloodshed. Such an attitude fits the mentality of youth in many civilizations. Anything would be better than what we now have, — what we need is a whole new start.

This Zealot option represented a real possibility, in fact, a real temptation for Jesus. It was this possibility to which He was particularly drawn in His debate with the tempter in the desert at His baptism, and again at His last trial in Gethsemane. More of His disciples came from the Zealot group than from any other part of Palestinian society, and their expectations were clearly along this line. Recent scholarship has clarified the extent to which Jesus' ministry must be understood as representing a constant struggle with the social option of revolutionary violence. This possibility was close enough to Jesus to constitute a genuine temptation.

He was perceived by some of His followers, and by the Herodians and Sadducees, as the nearest thing to a Zealot, and executed by the Romans on the grounds that He was one. He used their language, took sides with the poor as they did, condemned the same evils they did, created a disciplined community of committed followers as they did, prepared as they did to die for the divine cause.

Yet Jesus did not take the path of the Zealots. When the end finally came it was in fact one of the former Zealots on His team, Judas, who turned Him over to the authorities. He rejected this path not, as some of us might, because, being secure, we would stand to lose in a revolution, or because, being squeamish, we want to avoid social conflict. At those points He was with the Zealots.

His rejection of their righteous violence had another kind of reason. He did not agree that to use superior force or cunning to change society from the top down by changing its rulers, was the real need. What is wrong with the violent revolution according to Jesus is not that it changes too much but that it changes too little; the Zealot is the reflection of the tyrant whom he replaces by means of the tools of the tyrant. The Zealot resembles the tyrant whom he attacks in the moral claims he makes for himself and his cause: "In the world, kings lord it over their subjects; and those in authority are called their country's 'Benefactors'" (Lk. 22:25). One of the clear differences between Jesus and the Zealots was His readiness to associate with the impure, the sinner, the publican, the Roman. What is ultimately wrong, for Jesus, in the righteous arrogance of the revolutionary, is not the fact (which is historically demonstrable) that insurrectionary movements most often fail and thereby actually make worse the situation of the oppressed. Nor is the decisive failure the fact (also historically demonstrable and psychologically normal) that successful insurrectionary movements most often are corrupted by the temptations of the very appeal to righteousness in the use of power which brought them to victory. It is not even that most often (though perhaps less uniformly than for the other arguments) the revolutionary is immature, incapable of self-criticism, with little sense of history or of social determinants. If these were the only arguments against the Zealot model, they would convince an ethicist but they might not have convinced Jesus; they all leave the door open a crack for an exceptional case which might succeed after all.

What is wrong with the Zealot path for Jesus is not that it produces its new order by use of illegitimate instruments, but that the order it produces cannot be new. An order created by the *sword* is at the heart still not the new peoplehood Jesus announces. It still, by its subordination of persons (who may be killed if they are on the wrong side) to causes (which must triumph because they are right), preserves unbroken the self-righteousness of the mighty and denies the servanthood which God has chosen as His tool to remake the world.

But we are ahead of ourselves. Jesus had some other, less extreme, choices. He could have rejected the Roman rule and the compromises of the Herodians, without necessarily joining the Zealots.

A third logical possibility available to Jesus was the desert. He could withdraw from the tension and conflicts of the urban center where government and commerce constantly polluted even the most well-intentioned son of the law, seeking to find a place where He could be pure and perfectly faithful.

In the last decades we have come to know much more about the monasteries around the Dead Sea. These sizable colonies of people were doing just this; maintaining faithful copies of the text of the Old Testament Scriptures, living a life unspotted by the outside world and in literal conformity to the rabbinic rules.

There are some who have thought that this is the path of Christian faithfulness. The Amish, migrating every other generation, or the hippies in California canyons are only the extreme forms of such withdrawal. The rural community has often been praised as the place where it is easier to be Christian, because life is more simple and one has to deal with fewer people; the village has a minimum of government and all economic organizations are man-size.

The days of real rural withdrawal are fast passing, but the synthetic countryside we call the suburb, with its artificial old swimming holes, artificial expanses of meadow, and artificial campfire sites, set up to maintain an artificial distance from the city's problems, still represents some people's vision of what to live for. This is supplemented by the still more complete withdrawal of the weekend lakeside and the camping trailer. But Jesus, although His home was a village, found no hearing there, and left village life behind Him. He forsook His own handicraft and called His disciples away from their nets and their plows. He set out quite openly and consciously for the city and the conflict which was sure to encounter Him there.

There is yet a fourth possibility which, like the first, lay close on the path of Jesus. This was the option of "proper religion," represented in His society by the Pharisees. The Pharisees lived in the middle of urban society, yet they sought, like the desert sects, to keep themselves pure and separate. The root of the word "Pharisee" means "separate." They kept themselves pure in the midst of the city by keeping rules of segregation. Certain areas of life were to be avoided; certain elements of culture are not for the Pharisee. Certain coins, certain crops, certain persons, certain occupations, certain days were taboo.

So it is in our day; there are many who feel that it is both possible and desirable to distinguish by a clear line the "spiritual" or the "moral" issues, to which religion properly speaks, from "social" and "political" issues, which are not the business of religion. The theme of "revolution" in our society is the prime example of what is not the Christian's concern.

But the separation is really not that clean. To avoid revolution means to take the side of the establishment. To say that the church should not meddle with the problem of open housing is to conclude that the house owner and the real estate agent, even if members of the churches, receive no concrete moral guidance from beyond themselves. To say that it is not the business of the church to second guess the experts on details of political or military strategy, to have judgments on the moral legitimacy of particular laws, is to give one's blessing to whatever goes on. Those who object to the church's having something to say about economics, especially if that be critical of the existing capitalistic order, have no qualms about seeing the church on the other side of the economic question, or about economics having a say in the life of the churches.

So it comes as no surprise to be reminded that in the case of Jesus, the Pharisees as well, although deep moral and theological differences separated them from the Herodians and the Sadducees, finally did make common cause with them in the crucifixion because Jesus threatened their position of noninvolvement.

3. Light to the Nations

But what then is Jesus to do if He rejects at the same time the established order of the Herodians and the holy, violent revolution with which the Zealots sought to change that order: both the outward emigration of the Essenes and the inward emigration of the Pharisees? We need not meditate long to see that this question is our own.

To answer our question as it has been sharpened by a survey of available social strategies in Jesus' time and in ours, we must look back to what God had been doing or trying to do for a long, long time. The Bible story really begins with Abraham, the father of those who believe. Abraham was called to get up and leave Chaldea, the cultural and religious capital of the known world in his age, to go he knew not where, to find he knew not what. He could not know when or whether or how he could again have a home, a land of his own. And yet as he rose to follow this inscrutable promise, he was told that it was through him that the nations of the world would be blessed. In response Abraham promised his God that he would lead a different kind of life: a life different from the cultured and the religious peoples, whether urban or nomadic, among whom he was to make his pilgrim way.

"From the rocky heights I see them,
    I watch them from the rounded hills.
I see a people that dwells alone,
    that has not made itself one with the nations."
— Numbers 23:9

Yet in that apartness how present!

This is the original revolution; the creation of a distinct community with its own deviant set of values and its coherent way of incarnating them. Today it might be called an underground movement, or a political party, or an infiltration team, or a cell movement. The sociologists would call it an intentional community. Then they were called "Hebrews," a title which probably originally meant, "the people who crossed over."

Abraham's children did not always keep His promises, but God remained steadfast in His loyalty to them. His promises of righteousness to be brought to the nations through His servant Israel were from year to year reiterated, reinforced, clarified, even though the likelihood that the Israelites would become the instrument of their fulfillment seemed less and less evident. These were the promises, Christians believe, which Jesus came to keep.

Jesus did again what God had done in calling Abraham or Moses or Gideon or Samuel: He gathered His people around His word and His will. Jesus created around Himself a society like no other society mankind had ever seen:

1. This was a voluntary society: you could not be born into it. You could come into it only by repenting and freely pledging allegiance to its king. It was a society with no second generation members.

2. It was a society which, counter to all precedent, was mixed in its composition. It was mixed racially, with both Jews and Gentiles; mixed religiously, with fanatical keepers of the law and advocates of liberty from all forms; with both radical monotheists and others just in the process of disentangling their minds from idolatry; mixed economically, with members both rich and poor.

3. When He called His society together Jesus gave its members a new way of life to live. He gave them a new way to deal with offenders — by forgiving them. He gave them a new way to deal with violence — by suffering. He gave them a new way to deal with money — by sharing it. He gave them a new way to deal with problems of leadership — by drawing upon the gift of every member, even the most humble. He gave them a new way to deal with a corrupt society — by building a new order, not smashing the old. He gave them a new pattern of relationships between man and woman, between parent and child, between master and slave, in which was made concrete a radical new vision of what it means to be a human person. He gave them a new attitude toward the state and toward the "enemy nation."

At the heart of all this novelty, as we said already in explaining Jesus' response to the Zealot option, is what Jesus did about the fundamental human temptation: power. This was part of the promise:

"Here is my servant, whom I uphold,
  my chosen one in whom I delight,
I have bestowed my spirit upon him,
  and he will make justice shine on the nations.

He will not call out or lift his voice high,
　　or make himself heard in the open street.
He will not break a bruised reed,
　　or snuff out a smouldering wick;
he will make justice shine on every race,
　　never faltering, never breaking down,
he will plant justice on earth,
　　while coasts and islands wait for his teaching."
　　　　　　　　　　　　　　　　　— Isaiah 42:1-4

Jesus not only thought of Himself as doing somehow the work of this chosen "Servant"; He also saw this as His disciples' way.

You know that in the world,
　　rulers lord it over their subjects . . .
　　but it shall not be so with you.
Among you, whoever wants to be great must be your
　　　　servant . . .
　　like the Son of Man;
he did not come to be served, but to serve
and to give up his life as a ransom for many."
　　　　　　　　　　　　　　　　　— Matthew 20:25 ff.

All of this new peoplehood, the being-together with one another and the being different in style of life, His disciples freely promised to do, as He renewed the promise that through them the world should be blessed and turned rightside up.

Now the usual name for this new society which Jesus created is "church." But when we use the word "church" in our day we mean by it a gathering for worship, or the group of persons who gather for worship, or who might so gather, and who otherwise have little to do with each other. Sometimes it even means the building they meet in, or the organization which provides that there will be an officiant at the meeting, or even the national agency which manages the pension fund for the officiants' widows. But the word which Jesus used in the Aramaic language, like the equivalent word which the New Testament writers used in the Greek language, does not mean a gathering for worship nor an administration; it means a public gathering to deal with community business. Our modern terms *assembly, parliament, town meeting,* are the best equivalents. The church is not just a certain number of persons nor a specific gathering of persons assembled for a particular religious rite. The church is God's people gathered as a unit, as a people, gathered to do business in His name, to find what it means here and now to put into practice this different quality of life which is God's promise to them and to the world and their promise to God and service to the world.

Jesus did not bring to faithful Israel any corrected ritual or any new theories about the being of God. He brought them a new peoplehood and a new way of living together. The very existence of such a group is itself a deep social change. Its very presence was such a threat that He had to be crucified. But such a group is not only by its existence a novelty on the social scene; if it lives faithfully, it is also the most powerful tool of social change.

4. And Now?

"The kingdom of God is at hand: repent and believe the good news!" To repent is not to feel bad but to think differently. Protestantism, and perhaps especially evangelical Protestantism, in its concern for helping

31

every individual to make his own authentic choice in full awareness and sincerity, is in constant danger of confusing the kingdom itself with the benefits of the kingdom. If anyone repents, if anyone turns around to follow Jesus in his new way of life, this will do something for the aimlessness of his life. It will do something for his loneliness by giving him fellowship. It will do something for his anxiety and guilt by giving him a good conscience. So the Bultmanns and the Grahams whose "evangelism" is to proclaim the offer of restored selfhood, liberation from anxiety and guilt, are not wrong. If anyone repents, it will do something for his intellectual confusion, by giving him doctrinal meat to digest, a heritage to appreciate, and a conscience about telling it all as it is: So "evangelicalism" with its concern for hallowed truth and reasoned communication is not wrong; it is right. If a man repents it will do something for his moral weakness by giving him the focus for wholesome self-discipline, it will keep him from immorality and get him to work on time. So the Peales and the Robertses who promise that God cares about helping me squeeze through the tight spots of life are not wrong; they have their place. BUT ALL OF THIS IS NOT THE GOSPEL. This is just the bonus, the wrapping paper thrown in when you buy the meat, the "everything" which will be added, without our taking thought for it, if we seek first the kingdom of God and His righteousness!

The good news of God's original revolution is not, as the Zealots of right or left would say, that violence is only wrong when the bad guys use it, or that enmity is only wrong when it is violent. It does not say, with the emigrant to the desert, that you can cop out and do your own thing unmolested. It is not concerned with the inner-worldly emigration of the Pharisees, to refuse cooperation only at the point of personal complicity. It does not promise, with the Herodians and Sadducees, that if enough morally concerned people sign up to work for Dow, DuPont, and General Motors, we can beat the communists yet at feeding the world. All four of these classical strategies have in common that they dodge the duty of beginning now, first, with the creation of a new, voluntary, covenanting community in which the rejection of the Old is accredited by the reality of the New which has already begun.

The question for our time, in the world which awaits and aspires to revolution, is not whether the kingdom is coming but what we will do about it. It continues to be possible, and in fact likely, that we may choose the strategies which Jesus rejected. We could find most respectable company in any of these four camps, as did our fathers. Or we could, if we chose, accept in all its novelty and discover in all our creativity the kind of life together as fully human men among men which He came to live and to give, including the kind of death He came to die. We could accept, if we would repent, that novelty in our ways of dealing with one another, with ethnic differences, with social hierarchy, with money, with offenses, with leadership and with power, for which "revolutionary" is the only adequate word. "The kingdom of God is within your grasp: repent and believe the good news!"

II. THE POLITICAL AXIOMS
OF THE SERMON ON THE MOUNT*

We have begun our exposition of the ethic of discipleship with a portrayal of the ethical decisions made by
Jesus, whom the Christian disciple confesses as Lord.
This concrete portrayal of the realism of personal decision in historical conflict was indispensable to combat
one of the most widespread interpretations of the contemporary pacifist commitment: It is held that pacifism
proceeds from a logical, deductive, impersonal kind of
legalism taking certain biblical texts or certain ethical
principles with utmost rigor, without asking whether it
be possible or not to live up to such demanding ideals.
This is what many mean by "a Sermon-on-the-Mount
ethic."

It was important therefore to clarify first of all that
the human *career* of the Master is an interpretation of
and in fact the foundation of, His teaching: Any record
we have of the *teachings* of Jesus which we might seek
to *obey* is in its available form a full generation later

---

*Translated and rewritten from a lecture first presented in June, 1966,
to the Seminario Evangelico Menonita, Montevideo, Uruguay.

than the *events* and *decisions* which our first chapter recounted, and which Jesus' disciples followed. The Gospel writers could soberly record the accounts which we have, including the moral teachings which they record from the lips of Jesus, only because it was incontrovertible that He had lived and died just that way. We are thus still interpreting the person and work of Jesus when we read His moral teachings as these have been transmitted by the apostolic church.

We proceed as an early Christian convert would have, to the summary text which is now known as the Sermon on the Mount, and which must have served for those early converts as a kind of catechism. We have observed the impact of the man Jesus upon His society without asking why He took the path He did. What was it then which opened to Jesus the option of another way to relate to the needs of His oppressed people and the apparently evident options?

Our purpose is not to exposit in detail particular texts but to lift out those elements of logic, and the evidence of those axioms, which throw light especially on the novelty or uniqueness of the ethic of Jesus. It cannot be our concern to distinguish between the text we have and what the historical Jesus Himself really said. Neither need we renew the tired debates about how or whether a contemporary community can use a particular scriptural text in Christian ethics. We seek only to reflect the thought pattern of this primitive Christian catechism, for the light which it might throw first on why Jesus took the particular path we have seen He did, and derivatively, on why Christians today might find themselves behaving in ways very different from majority habits.

For our purposes we need not enter into the literary and critical debates about how this text came to be. [1] Nor need we search out at length the underlying issue of how ethical thinking went on in the early church, especially as this relates to the thinking of the Apostle Paul about the law, or to contemporary thinking about how it is possible systematically to deal with ethical issues. What we are now seeking is not an understanding of how the Sermon on the Mount could function as a new law in the church or in the revival of the church. [2] Nor is our concern very dependent upon knowing just how much of what Jesus is reported as saying here was never said before. [3] We seek simply to understand in its broadest and most axiomatic outlines, the widest framework within which Jesus spoke to moral issues. Our interest is, then, not in the detailed analysis of the Sermon on the Mount but in its structure and its logic, as these present a fundamental orientation capable of finding renewed expression in other cultures and ages as well.

This portrayal is undertaken in the full awareness of the doubts and challenges which must be faced by those who take it seriously; but a confrontation with those arguments is reserved for later portions of the book. Here we seek simply without debate or evaluation to describe the originality of this text in its coherence with the originality of the Teacher's career.

An Ethic of Repentance

Everything in the beginning chapters of Matthew's

Gospel is calculated to make clear that a new age of fulfillment is at hand. The genealogy, reaching back to the major landmarks of Israelite history, places the birth of Jesus right at the end of the third rounded cycle. The miraculous birth, surrounded by angelic announcements, was recognized by the astrologers from the East. The ministry of John the Baptist heralded the greater One about to appear. The baptism and the temptation revealed the future ministry of this Man. The calling of His disciples who in their number twelve, represented the claim to reconstitute Israel. All of this dramatized the proclamation that a new age was about to begin.

But for our purposes it is sufficient simply to record that Jesus began His own personal ministry by announcing the beginning of this age.

"From that day Jesus began to proclaim the message:
    'Repent; for the kingdom of Heaven is upon you.' "
                                            — Matthew 4:17

"He went round the whole of Galilee,
    teaching in the synagogues,
    preaching the gospel of the Kingdom,
    and curing whatever illness or infirmity there was
        among the people.
His fame reached the whole of Syria;
and sufferers from every kind of illness,
    racked with pain,
    possessed by devils, epileptic, or paralysed,
    were all brought to him, and he cured them.
Great crowds also followed him,
    from Galilee and the Ten Towns,
    from Jerusalem and Judaea,
    and from Transjordan."
                                        — Matthew 4:23-25

Repeating word for word the message of John the Baptist, Jesus says that the new age is dawning. Going beyond John, He demonstrates in signs and samples the healing power of the kingdom that has drawn near. The first and fundamental implication of this account is that we should expect Jesus to describe for His disciples a way of life which is new, unprecedented, surprising, perhaps even unacceptable to respectable men.

Centuries of church history, both in the penitential principles of Catholic tradition and in the concern of Protestantism for personal integrity, have taught us to misunderstand radically what John the Baptist and Jesus meant when they began preaching, "Repent! For the kingdom is at hand!" Under "repentance" we think of remorse, regret, sorrow for sin. But what they were calling for was a transformation of the understanding (*metanoia*), a redirected will ready to live in a new kind of world.

The teachings which follow refuse to measure by the standards of "common sense" or "realism" or "reason"; they testify to the novelty of the kingdom that is at hand. Jesus will therefore be describing for us a morality of repentance or of conversion; not a prescription of what every man can and should do to be happy; not a meditation on how best to guide a society, but a description of how a man behaves whose life has been transformed by meeting Jesus.

An Ethic of Discipleship

"When he saw the crowds he went up the hill. There he took his seat, and when his disciples had gathered round him he began to address them" (Mt. 5:1, 2). When Moses met God on a mountain and received from Him the tables of the law, this law was for all the children of Israel. When Jesus from another hill proclaims again the statutes of His rule, it is to His disciples. This is not a set of moral standards to be posed on everyone or on the unconvinced. It is not proposed that persons using these standards can rule the unbelieving world accordingly, nor that they will be prosperous and popular. The ethic of discipleship is not guided by the goals it seeks to reach, but by the Lord it seeks to reflect. It is no more interested in "success" or in "effectiveness" than He. It is binding only upon those voluntarily enrolled in the band of His followers. It is assumed that they will be a minority in society; how the world would look if everyone would behave as they is not a question we immediately need to answer.

The appeal which the thought of social upheaval has for many of the socially disadvantaged comes from a vision of the privilege that will be theirs under the new order. Often this vision is unrealistic. Especially in our day, many are experiencing that accession to the national sovereignty is not as simple a blessing as they had hoped when they were being colonized. Nevertheless one of the main motors of social change continues to be expectations of how acceptable the new order will be.

Jesus as well begins His moral revolution by announcing who it is that can rejoice in its coming:

"Blessed are the poor in spirit,
Blessed are the meek,

39

Blessed are the merciful."

— Matthew 5:1-7, RSV

With our heritage of moral bargaining, whether Catholic or Protestant, we have been led to misunderstand the "Beatitudes" as a scheme of performances and rewards. Be meek: then your reward will be to inherit the earth. Be pure in heart: your reward will be the vision of God. This misunderstanding arises when we separate the Beatitudes from the annunciation of the new regime. One cannot simply, by making up his mind, set out to "mourn" or to "be persecuted for righteousness' sake." Jesus is rather saying, "there are some who hunger and thirst after righteousness: *good for them!* For the kingdom is at hand and they shall be filled. There are those who make peace; *good for them!* for the kingdom is at hand and it will be known that they are sons of God." Christendom is not a matter of earning a place in the kingdom, nor is it a simple blind obedience to directions. It is not doing what we feel like, nor computing how to achieve the best results. It is loving in such a way that, when the kingdom approaches, we find ourselves among those who are "at home," who "fit" there, who are not out of place.

An Ethic of Testimony

"You are salt to the world.
And if salt becomes tasteless,
    how is its saltness to be restored?
It is now good for nothing
    but to be thrown away and trodden underfoot.

40

You are light for all the world.
A town that stands on a hill
    cannot be hidden.
When a lamp is lit,
    it is not put under the meal-tub,
    but on the lamp-stand,
    where it gives light to everyone in the house.
And you, like the lamp,
    must shed light among your fellows,
so that, when they see the good you do,
    they may give praise to your Father in heaven."
                                    — Matthew 5:13-16

The Christian church is to be a source of light and of savor. Not for her own glory, but to the praise of the Father, her good works are visible. They cannot be concealed. Her deeds are words. Later in the chapter Jesus asks of persons whose goodness is careful and calculating, "What reward can you expect?" (v. 46). In other words it is assumed that there should be something about the behavior of His disciples which will communicate to the world around.

Thus far we have been introducing ourselves into the framework of the teaching of Jesus, its presuppositions and its assumptions. But our goal is to grasp its substance, especially as it has to do with enemies, power, and war. This statement that the deeds of the church are a witness is a key thought. Our deeds must be measured not only by whether they fit certain rules, nor by the results they hope to achieve, but by what they "say."

What do I communicate to a man about the love of God by being willing to consider him an enemy? What do I say about personal responsibility by agreeing to consider him my enemy when it is only the hazard of birth that causes us to live under different flags? What do I say about forgiveness if I punish him for the sins of his rulers? How is it reconcilable with the gospel — good news — for the last word in my estimate of any man to be that, in a case of extreme conflict, it could be my duty to sacrifice his life for the sake of my nation, my security, or the political order which I prefer?

The idea that human life is intrinsically sacred is not a specifically Christian thought. But the gospel itself, the message that Christ died for His enemies, is *our* reason for being ultimately responsible for the neighbor's — and especially the enemy's — life. We can only say this to him if we say to ourselves that we cannot dispose of him according to our own will.

An Ethic of Fulfillment

> "You have learned that our forefathers were told. . . .
> But what I tell you is this."
>
> — Matthew 5:21 ff.

Such is the structure of the rest of the chapter. This has sometimes been interpreted as a rejection of the Old Testament in favor of a radically different set of demands. The Old Testament permitted hatred of the enemy — now Jesus demands that we love him. The oath, commanded then, is forbidden now. Just vengeance was required before; now it is rejected. And yet this passage opens with the promise that, "I have come not to destroy but to fulfill."

Let us not seek to solve the problem by the classical Protestant escape. Moving from another area of doctrine and another part of the New Testament, some Protestants have said that the "greater righteousness," exceeding that of the scribes and Pharisees, which Jesus here demands, is the gratuitous righteousness, the blamelessness before God, which is imputed to the believing sinner, "not by works lest any man should boast." This is the "fulfillment of the law" only in the sense that Christ is the end of the law; its demands, impossible to meet, crushing us under their impossibility, lead us to the faith which alone saves.

But if Jesus' purpose was to teach the uselessness of works for salvation, He hardly needed to be so precise about the novelty of His demands. For the Old Testament law was, from that perspective, already too much to bear. It needed no sharpening up. So this application of the doctrine of justification by faith alone is no answer; for the question it answers is a different one. This interpretation would understand Jesus to be criticizing the scribes and the Pharisees because they kept the law; but as a matter of fact Jesus is reprimanding them because they make it too easy to keep.

But perhaps the apparent contradiction between "fulfillment" and "but what I tell you" is not real. Is it actually the *law* which Jesus rejects as He speaks of enmity, of adultery, of swearing, and of vengeance? Does He take issue with either the text or the intent of the Torah?

In one case, Jesus directly contradicts the text which He quotes: "Love your neighbor and hate your enemy." Now "Love your neighbor" is in the law but "hate your enemy" is not. In two other cases, He lets the older statement stand unchanged, but intensifies enormously the application of its intention. The prohibition of murder and adultery remains; for Jesus to discern behind these forbidden acts the murderous or adulterous intention is no contradiction.

An understanding of the other three contrasts depends on what the earlier law actually intended. The provision for divorce (Deut. 24) as Jesus explains it more fully (Mt. 19) was a concession to "hardness of heart." But within that limitation, its effect was to defend the stability of a marriage and the dignity of women. Deuteronomy 24 does not approve of divorce; it does not even authorize it. It says that, where divorce has taken place already, the rejected and already remarried wife shall not be cheaply thrown around as if her second marriage bond had not constituted a breach of the first. This, the central concern of the earlier corrective, is what Jesus now carries to its consistent conclusion, namely that the second marriage, destroying the first, should not take place at all. Likewise the formula "eye for eye, tooth for tooth," in the ancient Israelite setting, actually meant a limitation placed upon vengeance. Vengeance could not be taken by the offended one or by the next of kin, but became the concern of the authorities, and was limited to the strict equivalent of the harm done. Thus even though Jesus pushes the renunciation of vengeance a powerful step further, it is in the direction set by the ancient rules. In a similar way, the same concern for veracity and for limiting the quasi-superstitious use of the name of God, which had *begun* by calling for truthfulness in swearing, takes a further step *in the same direction* by rejecting the oath itself as a concession to dishonesty and as an abuse of the name of God.

What Jesus meant by "fulfillment" was thus a quite literal filling full, a carrying on to full accomplishment of the intent of the earlier moral guides. It is therefore a most striking contrast, not to the Old Testament, but to its interpretation by current tradition; "righteousness of the scribes and Pharisees." Since the scribes and Pharisees were serious, pious, well-intentioned men like ourselves, trying as we do to get the moral teaching of their Scriptures out where it could give guidance to the common man, it is not a merely historical exercise to ask just what their mistake was. [4]

The first characteristic of the "righteousness of the scribes and Pharisees" is that it makes its standards fulfillable. Loving my neighbor is possible if I may still hate. Keeping rigorously an oath in the name of the Lord God Himself is possible if I may still leave room to cheat a little when I swear by Jerusalem or heaven. I can perhaps refrain from killing and from adultery if I may still cherish lustful and hateful thoughts. Thus we still seek to tailor our morals to fit our means, so that we can keep the rules and justify ourselves thereby. The logical circle is vicious. We want to be able to justify ourselves by what we can do; so we set our goals within reach. We construct for ourselves a manageable morality, which we can handle, without repentance, even if it should not be true that the kingdom of heaven is at hand.

This temptation is still with us, especially with regard to the problems of violence and national egoism which are our special concern here. One reason most theologies want to replace the Sermon on the Mount with some other standards is just this: they want something possible, something you can teach to all your children and require of all your parishioners, a goal a man can realistically reach. This is a very logical desire, if our goal is to be the moral mentors and "preachers" of a self-justifying civilization, including a service as chaplain to its armies. Jesus' criticism is only that this goal is not the same as being heralds of His kingdom.

The second trait of the "righteousness of the scribes and Pharisees" is that it is external, accessible. We get it out on the surface where we can prescribe and proscribe specific acts as right and wrong. We cannot tell if the heart is pure, but we can identify murder and adultery. We cannot make a man love one wife for life, but we can insist that the divorce proceedings be legal. Legitimacy replaces love as the standard.

Implied in the outwardness and fulfillability is a third characteristic. The righteousness of the scribes and Pharisees assumes a reasonable degree of legitimate self-interest. It can ask self-discipline but not self-denial; temperance or moderation, but not asceticism; it can ask us to bear a yoke but not a cross. And so it is today: the limits of moral rigor lie at the point of survival — national or personal. Do not lie — except to save your life or your country. Do not kill — except killers. Do not save yourself unless others depend on you. In the Protestant West it is traditional to accuse Roman Catholic confessional casuistry, and especially the Jesuits, of making too easy accommodations of the moral law to the needs and desires of man. But every tradition does this in one way or another.

An Ethic of Perfect Love

Three of the six examples Jesus gives, including the first and the last, are from the realm of enmity, violence, and vengeance. There is thus no violation of the central concern of Jesus if from here on we concentrate our attention on this area. The last verse of the chapter, and the portion which has contributed most to making the Sermon on the Mount a subject of systematic controversy, uses the word "perfect" in the older translations.

> "But what I tell you is this:
> Love your enemies and pray for your persecutors;
>   only so can you be children of your heavenly Father,
> who makes his sun rise on good and bad alike,
>   and sends the rain on the honest and the dishonest.
> If you love only those who love you,
>   what reward can you expect?
> Surely the tax-gatherers do as much as that.
> And if you greet only your brothers,
>   what is there extraordinary about that?
> Even the heathen do as much.
> There must be no limit to your goodness,
>   as your heavenly Father's goodness knows no bounds."
>   — Matthew 5:44-48

If everyone had read these verses more carefully, there would have been less fruitless speculation about whether and in what sense Christians can and should try to be, or expect to be "perfect." This command does make great problems in theology, and in the cure of souls if we take "perfect" to point to a goal of absolute flawlessness, or of having come to the end of all possibilities of growth. But Jesus is saying that we should not love only our friends because God did not

47

love only His friends. As the parallel statements in verse 45 and in Luke 6 make clear, we are asked to "resemble God" just at this one point: not in His omnipotence or His eternity or His impeccability, but simply in the undiscriminating or unconditional character of His love. [5] This is not a fruit of long growth and maturation; it is not inconceivable or impossible. We can do it tomorrow if we believe. We can stop loving only the lovable, lending only to the reliable, giving only to the grateful, as soon as we grasp and are grasped by the unconditionality of the benevolence of God. "There must be no limit to your goodness, as your heavenly Father's goodness knows no bounds."

This is one of the keys to the problem of war and legitimate defense. Every argument which would permit the taking of life is in one way or another based on calculations of rights and merits. I prefer the life of those nearest me to that of the foreigner; or the life of the innocent to that of the troublemaker, because — naturally, as everyone else does — my love is conditional, qualified, natural. Jesus does not condemn this normal self-seeking quality — for Gentiles — but He says there is nothing new, nothing special, nothing redemptive or healing about it — "What reward can you expect?" Not only is "perfect love" not limited to those who merit it; it even goes beyond the unjust demands of those who coerce compliance with their will. "Do not resist one who is evil. But if any one strikes you on the right cheek, turn to him the other also" (Mt. 5:39, RSV).

This is the origin of the label "nonresistance." The term is stronger and more precise than "nonviolence";

48

for one can hate or despise, conquer and crush another without the use of outward violence. But the term is confusing as well. It has been interpreted — by those who reject the idea — to mean a weak acceptance of the intentions of the evil one, resignation to his evil goals. This the text does not call for. The services to be rendered to the one who coerces us — carrying his burden a second mile, giving beyond the coat and cloak — are to his person, not to his purposes. The "resistance" which we renounce is a response in kind, returning evil for evil. [6] But the alternative is not complicity in his designs. The alternative is creative concern for the person who is bent on evil, coupled with the refusal of his goals.

What in the old covenant was a limit on vengeance — for one eye, only one eye — has now become a special measure of love demanded by concern for the redemption of the offender. This is "perfect love"; this is what it means that not a jot or a tittle will pass from the law until all is filled full.

An Ethic of Excess

The logic of the question we just saw Jesus putting is itself a pointer to the style of His disciple. "What do ye more than others?" (5:47, KJV) is for Jesus a fitting question whereas for the common discourse of ethics one measures oneself by others in order to measure up to the average. Here it is the excess, the going beyond what could be expected, the setting aside what one would have a right to, which is itself the norm. The reason for this is certainly not merely a concern to be visible (as we referred above to an ethical witness) nor can it be interpreted as the accumulation of some special kind of prestige or merit, which Jesus adequately sets aside as valid motivations. The point is rather that it is of the nature of the love of God not to let itself be limited by models or options or opportunities which are offered to it by a situation. It does more because the very event of exceeding the available models is itself a measure of its character. Far from asking as a certain contemporary style of ethics would, "What options does the situation give me?" or even more superficially, "What action does the situation demand?" Jesus would ask, "How in this situation will the life-giving power of the Spirit reach beyond available models and options to do a new thing whose very newness will be a witness to divine presence?"

An Ethic of Reconciliation

Jesus fulfills the meaning of "Thou shalt not kill" by moving to the level of personal intention: "Every one who gets angry with his brother shall be liable to judgment; everyone who says to his brother, **raca,** shall be answerable to the Sanhedrin; whoever says, 'thou fool!' (5:22, AV) shall be liable to the Gehenna of fire."

These three options are not simply Hebrew parallels, all saying the same thing. Significantly, the three punishments are of mounting severity, from the judgment of the local village elders, to the national Sanhedrin, and to the Gehenna of fire. At the same time the offense becomes more interior; from the spontaneous public expression of wrath to the more premeditated, more verbal, cold-blooded rejection of "thou fool."

The most serious hatred is seen not in the act but in the inner attitude toward the brother. Yet this is not the same thing which many moral thinkers mean when they speak of primacy of the "inner intention." In their thought, the idea is that if one's desire is that good may come of one's acts, or if one wishes to honor God, or if one is unselfish, then any action, including killing, can be right. But here the key "intention" is measured by the *brother*. One cannot even worship God, the text goes on to say, without being reconciled to the brother. [7] Jesus does not contrast the prohibition of killing on one hand and the love of neighbor on the other, so that for the sake of the principle of neighbor love one could kill. Jesus rather fulfills the intent of the prohibition of killing by centering it — not, as in Genesis 9, in the ritual sanctity of blood, nor, as in humanist philosophy, in the absolute value of the person; but in the fellowship between man and man, as a mirror and as means of fellowship with God.

Summary

We have only begun to read the Sermon on the Mount for light on the problem of war. We have not asked, as theological experts do, whether Jesus' command to turn the other cheek is a formal legal absolute, nor whether one can ever conceivably love his neighbor while taking his life. We have not asked whether these texts are the exact words of Jesus Himself, spoken in exactly this form on one particular day on one particular mountain, or whether they were put down in the present form out of the memories of the early church as a summary of His teachings. We have only observed the wider framework of Jesus' moral teaching; its dependence on the coming of the kingdom in His person and work; its expectation of novelty, of miracle, of visible witness; its derivation from the unqualified love of God; its unity of motive and deed. Seen in this light the love of neighbor, even the unqualified love of the neighbor, including the enemy, to the point of readiness to suffer unjustly at his hands, appears not only understandable but possible; not only possible but the most appropriate testimony to the nature of God's love and His kingdom.

We do not, ultimately, love our neighbor because Jesus told us to. We love our neighbor because God is like that. It is not because Jesus told us to that we love even beyond the limits of reason and justice, even to the point of refusing to kill and being willing to suffer — but because God is like that too.

Footnotes

1. The movement of scholarly consensus seems to converge in the conviction that the entire Gospel of Matthew, but especially its extended discourses, was preserved and transmitted by the earliest church for a rather specific catechetical function. Krister Stendahl, *The School of Matthew*, C. W. K. Gleerup, 1954, pp. 22 ff.; Philip Carrington, *The Primitive Christian Catechism*, Cambridge University Press, 1940, pp. 94 ff.

2. The antinomian mood of much ethical thought in our day must not stand in the way of recognizing situations where a conception of the renewing law of God has been a primary focus in the constituting and the renewing of God's people. The most sweepingly relevant example with regard to the Sermon on the Mount is its function in the renewal movements, both monastic and sectarian, of the late Middle Ages, as represented by Jerome and Luke of Prague and then by Peter Cheltchitzki and the Unitas Fratrum; cf. Geoffrey Nuttall, "The Law of Christ," in *Christian Pacifism in History*, Blackwell, 1958, pp. 15-31.

3. Misled by the recurrent phrase, "You have learned that our forefa-

thers were told. . . . But what I tell you is this," popular interpretation of the Sermon on the Mount has often described Jesus as opposed to the Jewish thought of His time. This is a serious misinterpretation which the present outline is not interested in fostering. What Jesus claimed to be representing was itself the best Jewish thought of the time, the culmination of the prophetic and rabbinic traditions which for centuries had been renewal movements within Hebrew society. Most of what He says has been said before. "You have learned that they were told" referred rather to narrow scholastic elaborations made to the law.

4. In our age many Christians, even those whose condemnation of Judaism was enshrined in ancient liturgy, are examining their tendency to misunderstand the Jews by seeing them only through the lens of a few polemic passages in the Gospels. On the basis of a broader historical analysis, one school of interpretation has concluded that Jesus arose and ministered within the Pharisaic wing of Judaism. The Sermon on the Mount is itself a document in the rabbinical and Pharisaic tradition. What Jesus labels here as "the righteousness of the Pharisees," we analyze as a universal human temptation and as a Christian temptation. We are not making a historical statement about Pharisaism in the first century, nor a judgmental statement about some peculiarly Jewish vice. Major strands of Protestant and Catholic thought have been more subject to it than normative Judaism has been.

5. One of the closest paraphrases is that of C. C. Torrey, "be all-including (in your goodwill) as your heavenly Father includes all." *The Four Gospels,* Harper, New York, 1933, p. 12.

6. There is serious scholarly opinion to the effect that this "resistance in kind" is meant specifically in reference to legal recourse against an evil which one has suffered. Cf. Stuart Currie: "Matthew 5:39; Resist or Protest?" *Harvard Theological Review,* April 1964, p. 140. The same interpretation was suggested by Tolstoy both for "resist not" in this text and for "judge not" in Matthew 7:1 ff. It is further a reinforcement of the instructions of 1 Corinthians 6:1 ff. As is spelled out by Paul, legal recourse as a response to an offense is questionable not only because it amounts to the recognition of the moral sovereignty of the pagan authorities. Such a concern to avoid court process, in a civilization where it must often have been very summary, is also advised by Jesus on simply pragmatic grounds (Mt. 5:2 ff.). It is thus not simply a dramatic specimen of a general ethical orientation: it is itself a part of the standard early Christian ethos.

7. This foundational reconciliation is described in two very brief anecdotal images: being with one's brother on the way to the court and being away from one's brother on the way to the temple. In both cases the imperative is simply to go and be reconciled to the brother.

Martin Niemoeller has pointed out that what is striking in both of these stories especially is that attention is not paid to the problem on which we would fix, namely who is right or wrong in the conflict. Our normal understanding of conflict resolution requires a prior judgment on who was right and who must apologize. Such an assumption is absent here. In either case it is up to me to restore the relationship, once in order that I may bring my sacrifice to God and once in order to stay out of prison. In both cases it appears that I am the guilty one, or at least that the court might judge me as such; a striking kind of accent to serve as an exposition of the inner meaning of "thou shalt not kill." "Thou shalt not kill" is thus sharpened not simply into "sustain life" but into "foster reconciliation at your own expense."

III. IF CHRIST IS TRULY LORD*

Christian thought is learning to give increasing attention to the importance of the Christian hope for the
Christian life. Christian thought in the decades prior
to the second World War was strongly influenced by
thinkers and preachers who hoped for the brotherhood
of man just around the corner and who therefore
thought they had no time to waste on eschatology. The
very word frightened them; it seemed to suggest weird
speculations and wild-eyed fanatics out of touch with
the world's real needs. And yet for all their down-to-
earth social concern and their avoidance of date-set-
ting, these optimists and believers in man also had an
eschatology. Their simple confidence that they could be
sure of the meaning of life was in itself a doctrine of
what is ultimate — i.e., an eschatology — though a
questionable one, being in part unconscious and not

---

*Paper presented to a Theological Study conference at Heerenwegen,
Zeist, (The Netherlands) in May, 1954. Since reproduced as a pamphlet in the
Concern reprint series, Scottdale, Pennsylvania. The text is left substantially
in the form of the first pamphlet printing (1959). Footnotes were added in
1970. The original title was *Peace Without Eschatology?*

directly based on Christian foundations.

The plan of the World Council of Churches to set the Christian hope in the center of its theological deliberations at Evanston [1] is a recognition that history and human endeavor can be understood only in terms of God's plan. There is no significance to human effort and, strictly speaking, no history unless life can be seen in terms of ultimate goals. The *eschaton,* the "Last Thing," the End-Event, imparts to life a meaningfulness which it would not otherwise have.

A singularly apt example of the eschatological mode of thought is the use of the term "peace" to designate the position of the conscientious objector or of the "Historic Peace Churches." "Peace" is not an accurate description of what has generally happened to nonresistant Christians throughout history, nor of the way the conscientious objector is treated in most countries today. Nor does Christian pacifism guarantee a warless world. "Peace" describes the pacifist's hope, the goal in the light of which he acts, the character of his action, the ultimate divine certainty which lets his position make sense; it does not describe the external appearance or the observable results of his behavior. This is what we mean by eschatology: a hope which, defying present frustration, defines a present position in terms of the yet unseen goal which gives it meaning. Our task here is to examine the relation between the present position and the goal, between pacifism and "peace," in the basis of the biblical eschatology.

We must first of all distinguish between *eschatology* — whose concern as we have defined it is the meaning of the *eschaton* for present history — and *apocalyptics*

— the effort to obtain precise information as to the date and shape of things to come. In marked contrast to the apocryphal literature of the time, the Bible is far more interested in eschatology than in apocalyptics; even when an apocalyptic type of literature occurs, its preoccupation is not with prediction for the sake of prediction, but rather with the meaning which the future has for the *present*. It would be inaccurate to maintain that an apocalyptic interest is foreign to New Testament Christianity, but we may nevertheless carry on our present study without asking the questions which the apocalypses answer.

Recent New Testament study has devoted itself to lifting out of the records of the life of the first churches the content of the *kerygma*, the central message of the apostolic preachers. The message is no timeless theological statement; it is from beginning to end eschatological, a declaration about events and their place in the unfolding of God's purpose. It would be a rewarding study to analyze the various stages of salvation history — the backward look to David and the prophets of old, the recital of the works of Christ, His passion and resurrection, the forward look to His coming in preparation for which all men must repent[2] — for each stage has a particular significance for ethics. We must, however, limit our present study to our age, which extends from the resurrection to the final coming. In this framework we shall seek the answer to two questions: how shall we understand attempts to build "peace without eschatology," i.e., to build a strategy for Christians in society upon a wrong understanding of eschatology? and how does a biblical eschatology clarify the place and meaning of Christian pacifism? The biblical emphases are generally accepted by contemporary theologians of all schools of thought.

Peace with Eschatology: Nonresistance and the Aeons

The New Testament sees our present age — the age of the church, extending from Pentecost to the Parousia — as a period of the overlapping of two aeons. These aeons are not distinct periods of time, for they exist simultaneously. They differ rather in nature or in direction; one points backwards to human history outside of (before) Christ; the other points forward to the fullness of the kingdom of God, of which it is a foretaste. Each aeon has a social manifestation: the former in the "world," the latter in the church or the body of Christ.

The new aeon came into history in a decisive way with the incarnation and the entire work of Christ. Christ had been awaited eagerly by Judaism for centuries; but when He came He was rejected, for the new aeon He revealed was not what men wanted. The Jews were awaiting a new age, a bringing to fulfillment of God's plan; but they expected it to confirm and to vindicate all their national hopes, prides, and solidarities. Thus Christ's claims and His kingdom were to them scandalous.

The new aeon involves a radical break with the old; Christ also was forced to break with the Jewish national community to be faithful to His mission. The gospel He brought, even though expressed in terms borrowed from politics *(kingdom)* and involving definite consequences for the social order, proclaimed the institution of a new kind of life, not of a new government. All through His ministry, from the temptation in the desert to the last minute in Gethsemane, political means were offered Him from all sides as short cuts to the accomplishment of His purposes, and He refused to use them. He struck at the very institution of human justice with His "Who made me a judge over you?" and even into the intimacy of the family circle with His "not peace but a sword!" Students of the Bible have in the past given inadequate attention to this aspect of Jesus' attitude; for our present problem it is of utmost significance to be aware that human community (as it exists under the sign of the old aeon) was far from being Jesus' central concern. [3]

Jesus' interest was in man; the reason for His low esteem for the political order was His high, loving esteem for man as the concrete object of His concern. Christ is *agape;* self-giving, nonresistant love. At the cross this nonresistance, including the refusal to use political means of self-defense, found its ultimate revelation in the uncomplaining and forgiving death of the innocent at the hands of the guilty. This death reveals how God deals with evil; here is the only valid starting point for Christian pacifism or nonresistance. The cross is the extreme demonstration that *agape* seeks neither effectiveness nor justice, and is willing to suffer any loss or seeming defeat for the sake of obedience.

But the cross is not defeat. Christ's obedience unto death was crowned by the miracle of the resurrection and the exaltation at the right hand of God.

"Bearing the human likeness,
revealed in human shape,

he humbled himself, and in obedience
accepted even death — death on a cross.
Therefore God raised him to the heights
and bestowed on him the name above all names. . . ."

— Philippians 2:8-10

Effectiveness and success had been sacrificed for the sake of love, but this sacrifice was turned by God into a victory which vindicated to the utmost the apparent impotence of love. The same life of the new aeon which was revealed in Christ is also the possession of the church, since Pentecost answered the Old Testament's longings for a "pouring out of the Spirit on all flesh" [4] and a "law written in the heart." [5] The Holy Spirit is the "down payment" on the coming glory and the new life of the resurrection is the path of the Christian now. But before the resurrection there was the cross, and the Christian must follow his Master in suffering for the sake of love.

Nonresistance is thus not a matter of legalism but of discipleship, not "thou shalt not" but "as he is so are we in this world" (1 Jn. 4:17, RSV), and it is especially in relation to evil that discipleship is meaningful. Every strand of New Testament literature testifies to a direct relationship between the way Christ suffered on the cross and the way the Christian, as disciple, is called to suffer in the face of evil (Mt. 10:38; Mk. 10:38 f.; 8:34 f.; Lk. 14:27). Solidarity with Christ ("discipleship") must often be in tension with the wider human solidarity. (Jn. 15:20; 2 Cor. 1:5; 4:10; Phil. 1:29; 2:5-8; 3:10; Col. 1:24 f.; Heb. 12:1-4; 1 Pet. 2:21 f.; Rev. 12:11). [6]

It is not going too far to affirm that the new thing

revealed in Christ was this attitude to the old aeon, including force and self-defense. The cross was not in itself a new revelation; Isaiah 53 foresaw already the path which the Servant of Jahweh would have to tread. Nor was the resurrection essentially new; God's victory over evil had been affirmed, by definition one might say, from the beginning. Nor was the selection of a faithful remnant a new idea. What was centrally new about Christ was that these ideas became incarnate. But superficially the greatest novelty and the occasion of stumbling was His willingness to sacrifice, in the interest of nonresistant love, all other forms of human solidarity, including the legitimate national interests of the chosen people. The Jews had been told that in Abraham all the nations would be blessed and had understood this promise as the vindication of their nationalism. Jesus revealed that the contrary was the case: the universality of God's kingdom contradicts rather than confirms all particular solidarities and can be reached only by first forsaking the old aeon. (Lk. 18:28-30.)

In the Old Testament the prophets had been lonely men, cut off from their people by their loyalty to God (which was, in the deepest sense, their real loyalty to their people, even though the people condemned them as troublemakers). Then in the New Testament the body of Christ came into being, a new people in the prophets' line, replacing disobedient Israel as the people of the promise. [7] Nationalism and pragmatism are both rejected in the life of the people of the new aeon, whose only purpose is love in the way of the cross and in the power of the resurrection.

Christ is not only the Head of the church; He is at the same time Lord of history, reigning at the right hand of God over the principalities and powers. The old aeon, representative of human history under the mark of sin, has also been brought under the reign of Christ (which is not identical with the consummate kingdom of God. 1 Cor. 15:24). The characteristic of the reign of Christ is that evil, without being blotted out, is channelized by God, in spite of itself, to serve His purposes. Vengeance itself, the most characteristic manifestation of evil, instead of creating chaos as is its nature, is harnessed through the state in such a way as to preserve order and give room for the growth and work of the church. Vengeance is not thereby redeemed or made good; it is nonetheless rendered subservient to God's purposes, as an anticipation of the promised ultimate defeat of sin.

This lordship over history had already been claimed for Jahweh in the Old Testament. Isaiah 10 exemplifies God's use of the state's vengefulness to administer His judgment, but without approving of the vengefulness, and without exempting the "scourge of His wrath" from judgment in its turn. When the New Testament attributes this lordship over history and the powers to Christ, it means that the essential change which has taken place is not within the realm of the old aeon, vengeance and the state, where there is really no change; it is rather that the new aeon revealed in Christ takes primacy over the old, explains the meaning of the old, and will finally vanquish the old. The state did not change with the coming of Christ; what changed was the coming of the new aeon which proclaimed doom of the old one.

Romans 13 and the parallel passages in 1 Timothy 2 and 1 Peter 2 give us the criteria for judging to what extent a state's activities (since the state incarnates this semisubdued evil) are subject to Christ's reign. If the use of force is such as to protect the innocent and punish the evildoers, to preserve peace so that "all men might come to the knowledge of the truth," then that state may be considered as fitting within God's plan, as subject to the reign of Christ. This positive evaluation cannot apply to a given state in all that it does, but at best in one case at a time, each time it chooses the best alternative rather than adding evil to evil. It is, however, possible, and even frequent, for a state to abandon this function, to deny any sort of submission to a moral order higher than itself, and in so doing to punish the innocent and reward the guilty. That state is what we find in Revelation 13, best described as demonic. Pilate condemning Jesus, not daring to be honest with his own recognition of Jesus' innocence, shows the weak form of this disobedience; the strong form is sufficiently well known in our day to need no further description.

Cullmann describes the subjugation of the old aeon in terms of "D-Day" and "V-Day." D-Day, the successful invasion of the continent of Europe by the Allied forces, was the decisive stroke which determined the end of World War II. Yet the war was not over. Between the decisive stroke and the final surrender (V-Day) there was a period in which the Axis powers were fighting a losing battle and the Allies were relatively sure of final triumph. This corresponds to the age of the church. Evil is potentially subdued, and its submission is already a reality in the reign of Christ, but the final triumph of God is yet to come.

The consummation will mean the fulfillment of the new aeon and the collapse of the old. The "world" in the sense of creation becomes after purgation identical with the new aeon, after having been the hostage of the old. It is in the light of this promised fulfillment that life in the new aeon, which seems so ineffective now, is nevertheless meaningful and right.

The consummation is first of all the vindication of the way of the cross. When John weeps in despair because there is no one to break the seals of the scroll in which is revealed the meaning of history, his joy comes from the cry that the Lamb that was slain is worthy to take the scroll and open its seals (first vision, Rev. 5), for the Lamb has ransomed men of every nation to make them a kingdom of servants of God who shall reign on earth. The ultimate meaning of history is to be found in the work of the church. (This relationship of Christ's suffering to His triumph is also stated in Philippians 2; the centrality of the church in history in Titus 2 and 1 Peter 2.) The victory of the Lamb through His death seals the victory of the church. Her suffering, like her Master's, is the measure of her obedience to the self-giving love of God. Nonresistance is right, in the deepest sense, not because it works, but because it anticipates the triumph of the Lamb that was slain.

The apparent complicity with evil which the nonresistance position involves has always been a stumbling block to nonpacifists. Here we must point out that this

attitude, leaving evil free to be evil, leaving the sinner free to separate himself from God and sin against
man, is part of the nature of *agape* itself, as revealed
already in creation. If the cutting phrase of Peguy,
"complice, c'est pire que coupable," were true, then
God Himself must needs be the guilty one for making
man free and again for letting His innocent Son be
killed. The modern tendency to equate involvement
with guilt should have to apply *par excellence*, if it
were valid at all, to the implication of the all-power-
ful God in the sin of His creatures. God's love for men
begins right at the point where He permits sin against
Himself and against man, without crushing the rebel
under his own rebellion. The word for this is divine
patience, not complicity.

But this gracious divine patience is not the complete
answer to evil. We have seen that evil is already
brought into check by the reign of Christ; the consummation of this reign is the defeat of every enemy by
the exclusion of evil. Just as the doctrine of creation
affirms that God made man free and the doctrine of redemption says this freedom of sin was what led *agape*
to the cross, so also the doctrine of hell lets sin free,
finally and irrevocably, to choose separation from God.
Only by respecting this freedom to the bitter end can
love give meaning to history; any universalism which
would seek, in the intention of magnifying redemption,
to deny to the unrepentant sinner the liberty to refuse
God's grace would in reality deny that human choice
has any real meaning at all. With judgment and hell
the old aeon comes to its end (by being left to itself)
and the fate of the disobedient is exclusion from the

new heaven and new earth, the consummation of the new society which began in Christ.

It is abundantly clear in the New Testament, as all exegetes agree, that this final triumph over evil is not brought about by any human or political means. The agent in judgment is not the church, for the church suffers nonresistantly. (Note the themes of *patience* and *endurance* in Revelation 6:9-11; 13:10; 14:12.) Nor is the agent the state, as it is for the judgments of God within history; for in fact the state, refusing ever more demonically Christ's dominion, becomes God's major enemy (Antichrist). God's agent is His own miraculous Word, the sword coming from the mouth of the King of kings and Lord of lords who is astride the white horse (Rev. 19). Just as has been the case ever since the patriarchs, and most notably at Christ's cross, the task of obedience is to obey and the responsibility for bringing about victory is God's alone, His means beyond human calculation. God's intervention, not human progress, is the vindication of human obedience. The Christian's responsibility for defeating evil, is to resist the temptation to meet it on its own terms. To crush the evil adversary is to be vanquished by him because it means accepting his standards.

The term "interim ethics" has often been used to describe the ethics of the New Testament. Customarily (according to the line of thought credited to Albert Schweitzer) this term means that Christ and the New Testament writers were led by their expectancy of an early end of time to an irresponsible attitude to ethics in society. This analysis springs from the attempt to judge on the basis of the old aeon. The New Testament

66

view is rather : "Were you not raised to life with Christ? Then aspire to the realm above" (Col. 3:1). It means being longsighted, not shortsighted; it means trusting God to triumph through the cross. Faith is just this attitude (as the examples of Heb. 11:1 — 12:4 show), the willingness to accept the apparently ineffective path of obedience, trusting in God for the results. Faith, even in Hebrews 11:1 f., does not mean doctrinal acquiescence to unproved affirmations, but the same trust in God which Christ initiated and perfected in itself (12:3). Again the example is the cross, which was right in itself even though its rightness (in terms of ultimate effect) was not yet apparent.

Peace Without Eschatology: the Constantinian Heresy

We have seen that the eschatological situation — in which nonresistance is meaningful and in which the state has its place — is one of tension between two aeons, tension which will be resolved by the triumph of the new in the fullness of the kingdom of God. The attitude which seeks peace without eschatology is that which would identify church and world, or fuse the two aeons in the present age without the act of God whereby evil is removed from the scene. This means a confusion between the providential purpose of the state, that of achieving a "tolerable balance of egoisms" (an expression borrowed with gratitude from Reinhold Niebuhr) and the redemptive purpose of the church, the rejection of all egoism in the commitment to discipleship. This confusion leads to the paganization of the church and the demonization of the state.

The common understanding of religion in the ancient Middle East was that of the tribal deity; a god whose significance was not ethical but ceremonial. His purpose was not to tell his people how to live, but to support their tribal unity and guarantee their prosperity through the observance of the proper cultic rites. This pagan attitude came to light in Israel as well in the form of the false prophets, whose significance in Old Testament times we often underestimate. Whereas the true prophets of the Lord proclaimed Jahweh's ethical requirements, His judgment, and His call to repentance, the false prophets were supported by the state in return for their support of the state's projects. Rather than define ethical demands of God, they committed God to the approval of the king's own plans. Jeremiah resumed their service as being to proclaim: "peace" when there is no peace, i.e., proclaiming peace without judgment, peace with eschatology. This position was far from pacifism. "Shalom," "peace" as the false prophets preached it, referred not to the absence of war but to the blessing of God on national aims, including wars for national interest (Jer. 6:13-15; 8:7-14). The false prophets, making God to be a handyman rather than a judge, thus inaugurated the line of those who seek to sanctify nationalism with the name of God. This line goes on into the Maccabees and to the various parties of Jesus' time who attempted to unite faith and nationalism in various ways — the Sadducees by collaboration, the Zealots by rebellion. Jesus, in close contact with the Zealots' movement, consistently refused their intention to wage war for national independence. [8]

The classic expression of this attitude in the Christian epoch is known as *Constantinianism;* the term refers to the conception of Christianity which took shape in the century between the Edict of Milan and the *City of God.* The central nature of this change, which Constantine himself did not invent nor force upon the church, is not a matter of doctrine nor of polity; it is the identification of church and world in the mutual approval and support exchanged by Constantine and the bishops. The church is no longer the obedient suffering line of the true prophets; she has a vested interest in the present order of things and uses the cultic means at her disposal to legitimize that order. She does not preach ethics, judgment, repentance, separation from the world; she dispenses sacraments and holds society together. Christian ethics no longer means the study of what God wants of man; since all of society is Christian (by definition, i.e., by baptism), Christian ethics must be workable for all of society. Instead of seeking sanctification, ethics becomes concerned with the persistent power of sin and the calculation of the lesser evil; at the best it produces puritanism, and at the worst simple opportunism.

It is not at all surprising that Augustine, for whom the Constantinian church was a matter of course, should have held that the Roman church was the millennium. Thus the next step in the union of church and world was the conscious abandon of eschatology. This is logical because God's goal, the conquest of the world by the church, had been reached (via the conquest of the church by the world). By no means did Augustine underestimate the reality of sin; but he seriously overestimated the adequacy of the available institutional and sacramental means for overcoming it.

This reasoning goes one step further. If the kingdom is in the process of realization through the present order, then the state is not simply a means of reconciling competing egoisms in the interest of order; it can be an agent of God's defeat of evil and may initiate disorder. The Crusades are the classic case. Rather than preserving peace, which 1 Timothy 2 asserts is the purpose of kings, the Holy Roman Empire wages war for the faith and against the heathen. Thus the function of judgment which the New Testament eschatology leaves to God, becomes also the prerogative of the state, with the church's consent, if not urging.

Herbert Butterfield, in his study *Christianity, Diplomacy, and War* demonstrates that the periods of relative stability and cultural advance have been those where wars were limited to pragmatic local adjustments between conflicting interests (in which case they could be somehow compared to the police function and considered as subject to the reign of Christ). Likewise, the least social progress has come when nations, in a Constantinian attitude, have felt obligated by honor to fight for a "cause." The Thirty Years' War and the ideological wars of our century are good examples. In these cases the use of force, by claiming to be a positive good rather than an evil subdued by Christ, becomes demonic and disrupts the stability of society more than it serves it. No longer subject to the restraint of Christ, the state, blessed by the church, becomes plaintiff, judge, jury, and executioner; and the rightness of the cause justifies any methods, even the suppression or extermination of the enemy. Thus even the New Testa-

70

ment doctrine of hell finds its place in Constantinianism; the purpose of exterminating, rather than subduing, evil is shifted from the endtime to the present. Standing not far from the brink of a world crusade to end all crusades, we do well to remember that the Constantinian and crusader's mentality is, far from being a way to serve Christ's kingdom, a sure road to demonizing the state by denying the limits to its authority and failing to submit its claims to a higher moral instance.

Constantinianism was at least consistent with its starting point; it knew only one society, that of the Roman empire, and sought to Christianize it. But today nations are numerous, and each nation takes over for itself the authority from God to represent the cause of history. We must yet seek the origin of this kind of nationalism in the example of Constantine. For Constantine, in replacing Christ's universal reign by the universal empire, shut out the barbarians. This seemed quite normal, since they were not Christian; but in reality it gave the church's sanction to the divided state of the human community, and opened the door to the concept that one nation or people or government can represent God's cause in opposition to other peoples who, being evil, need to be brought into submission. When the Germanic tribes replaced the Empire they applied this sense of divine mission to their tribal interests, despite all the efforts of the medieval church toward maintaining peace. Once admitted in principle, this attitude could later bless nationalism just as consistently as it had blessed imperialism. The universality of Christ's reign is replaced by the particularism of a specific state's intentions.

This goes even further. Once it is admitted that a particular group egoism is the bearer of the meaning of history, so that the nation's or the group's cause is endorsed by God, the divisiveness thus authorized does not stop with nationalism. Just as the medieval unity of Europe broke down into autonomous kingdoms each claiming God's sanction, so also each nation now tends to break down into classes and parties, each of them again sure of divine approval or its secular equivalent. Once a "cause" justifies a crusade or national independence, it may just as well justify a revolution, a cold war threatening to grow hot, or the toppling of a cabinet to suit a particular party's interest. All these phenomena, from the Bolshevik Revolution to John Foster Dulles, are examples of one basic attitude. They suppose that it is justified in the interest of a "cause" for a particular group, whose devotion to that cause is a special mission from God, to rend the fabric of human solidarity, poisoning the future and introducing a rupture which is the precise opposite of the "peace" which it is the duty of the state under the lordship of Christ to insure.

If, with the New Testament, we understand the unity of the church as a universal bond of faith, we can understand that the real sectarianism, in the biblical sense of unchristian divisiveness, was the formation of churches bound to the state and identified with the nation. And on the other hand, some so-called "sects," notably the 16th-century Anabaptists, the 17th-century Quakers, the 18th-century Moravians, and the 19th-century Open Brethren, were by their freedom from such ties, by their mobility and their missionary concern, by their preference of biblicism and obedient faith to creedal orthodoxy, the veritable proponents of ecumenical Christianity. On the other hand, the revolution of Münster, with which uninformed historians still blacken the Anabaptist name, was not consistent Anabaptism; it was a reversion to the same heresy accepted by Lutherans and Catholics alike — the belief that political means can be used against God's enemies to oblige an entire society to do God's will. It is for this reason that the nonresistant Anabaptists denounced the Münsterites even before the conversion of Menno. Münster attempted, just as did Constantine, to take into human hands the work which will be done by the Word of God at the end of the age — the final victory of the church and defeat of evil.

One of the startling manifestations of modern particularized Constantinianism is the parallelism between the opposing groups, each of which claims to be right. In our day the examples are as patent as they were in the Thirty Years' War. Both Dulles and Molotov were convinced that no co-existence of two opposing systems was possible; each was willing not only to wage war but even to destroy all culture rather than let the enemy exist. Each was sure that the other was the aggressor and that any injustices or inconsistencies on one's own side (like the police methods in the people's democracies or the West's support of Rhee, Tito, Franco, French colonialism) were only rendered necessary by the enemy's aggressiveness and espionage. Each was convinced that history is on the side of his system and that the opposing system is the incarnation of evil. Each was willing to have the people's morale upheld by the churches; neither was willing to stand under God's judgment and neither felt the need to repent. Each felt obliged to take God's plan into his own hands and guaranteed the triumph of the good by means of the available economic, political, and if need be military weapons. Each sought peace by the use of force in the name of God without accepting God's judgment, without abandoning group egoism, without trusting God to turn obedience into triumph by His own means. In short, both were right where Israel was in the time of Micaiah, and both were amply served by churches faithful to the tradition of the four hundred prophets of 1 Kings 22. "Attack," they answered, "the Lord will deliver it into your hands" (v. 7). Peace without eschatology has become war without limit; thus is fulfilled the warning of the Lord, "Satan cannot be cast out by Beelzebub."

Eschatology and the Peace Witness

Having seen how the crusader's thesis that the end justifies the means is finally self-defeating, and that the Constantinian heresy ultimately reverts to a purely pagan view of God as a tribal deity, we must return to the New Testament eschatology for a new start. We shall ask not only what is required of Christians (for on this level the imperative of nonresistance is clear) but also whether any guidance may be found in the realm of social strategy and the prophetic witness to the state. Certain aspects of a biblical, eschatological, nonresistant Christian view of history may be sketched here.

First of all, we must admit that only a clearly eschatological viewpoint permits a valid critique of the present historical situation and the choice of action which can be effective. Noneschatological analysis of history is unprotected against the dangers of subjectivism and opportunism, and finishes by letting the sinful present situation be its own norm. History, from Abraham to Marx, demonstrates that significant action, for good or for evil, is accomplished by those whose present action is illuminated by an eschatological hope. There are some kinds of apocalypticism which may favor a do-nothing attitude to social evil; this is precisely what is unchristian and unbiblical about some kinds of apocalypticism. But Schweitzer's thesis, generally accepted by liberal theologians, that the eschatological expectancy of the early church led to ethical irresponsibility, is simply wrong, exegetically and historically.

Within pacifist circles there is urgent need to clear up a serious ambiguity in the understanding of our peace witness. This ambiguity contributed to the weakness of the optimistic political pacifism of the Kellogg-Briand era, and was really a Constantinian attitude, as it felt that true peace was about to be achieved in our time by unrepentant states. Once again the hope was for peace without eschatology.

Restoring our peace witness to its valid eschatological setting, we find it to have three distinct elements. One is addressed to Christians: "Let the church be the church!" As *Peace Is the Will of God* [9] attempts to do it, we must proclaim to every Christian that pacifism is not the prophetic vocation of a few individuals, but that every member of the body of Christ is called to absolute nonresistance in discipleship and to abandonment of all loyalties which counter that obedience, including the desire to be effective immediately or to make oneself responsible for civil justice. This is the call of the Epistle to the Hebrews — a call to faith and sanctification. Eschatology adds nothing to the content of this appeal; but the knowledge that the way of the Lamb is what will finally conquer demonstrates that the appeal, for all its scandal, is not nonsense.

Second, there is the call to the individual, including the statesman, to be reconciled with God. This is evangelism in the strict contemporary sense, and is a part of the peace witness. Any social-minded concern which does not have this appeal to personal commitment at its heart is either utopian or a polite form of demagoguery. But we must still face the problem with which we began. What is our witness to the statesman, who is not in the church and has no intention to be converted? Here only the eschatological perspective can provide an answer, whereas the "realisms" which agree with Constantine finish by giving him a free hand. We must return to the first Christian confession of faith, *Christos kyrios*, Christ is Lord. The reign of Christ means for the state the obligation to serve God by encouraging the good and restraining evil, i.e., to serve peace, to preserve the social cohesion in which the leaven of the gospel can build the church, and also render the old aeon more tolerable.

Butterfield, not a pacifist but an honest historian, applies this sort of viewpoint to the question of war. He concludes that the Constantinian war, i.e., the crusade whose presupposition is the impossibility of co-existence and whose aim is unconditional surrender, is not only bad Christianity but also bad politics. He concludes with a qualified approval of what he calls "limited war," i.e., war which is the equivalent of a local police action, aiming not at annihilation but at a readjustment of tensions within the framework of an international order whose existence is not called into question. His thesis is that this sort of balance-of-power diplomacy which one associates with the Victorian age is the most realistic. In virtue of its recognition that it is not the kingdom of God, it is able to preserve a proximate justice which permits the silent growth of what Butterfield calls the "imponderables," those attitudes and convictions, not always rational or conscious, which are the real preservatives of peace. These factors of cohesion: ideals of brotherhood, of honesty, of social justice, or the abundant life, are the by-products of the Christian witness and the Christian home, and have leavening effect even on non-Christians and non-Christian society. It would even be possible to speak of a limited doctrine of progress within this context. As long as the state does not interfere, either through fascism or through violence which destroys the tissue of society, these by-products of Christianity do make the world, even the old aeon, immensely more tolerable. Yet they make men ultimately no better in the sight of God, and no better administrators of the talents entrusted them.

The function of the state is likened by Butterfield to the task of the architect in building a cathedral. The force of gravity, like human egoism, is not in itself a constructive force. Yet if art and science combine to shape and place properly each stone, the result is a unity of balanced tensions, combining to give an impression not of gravity but of lightness and buoyancy. This sort of delicate balance of essentially destructive forces is what the political apparatus is to maintain under the lordship of Christ, for the sake not of the cathedral but of the service going on within it.

Thus the church's prophetic witness to the state rests on firmly fixed criteria; every act of the state may be tested according to them and God's estimation pronounced with all proper humility. The good are to be protected, the evildoers are to be restrained, and the fabric of society is to be preserved, both from revolution and from war. Thus, to be precise, the church can condemn methods of warfare which are indiscriminate in their victims and goals of warfare which go further than the localized readjustment of a tension. These things are wrong for the state, not only for the Christian. On the other hand, a police action within a society or under the United Nations cannot on the same basis be condemned on principle; the question is whether the safeguards are there to insure that it become nothing more. In practice, these principles would condemn all modern war, not on the basis of perfectionist discipleship ethics, but on the realistic basis of what the state is for.

Two comments must be appended here. First of all, the kind of objectivity which makes it possible to see the task of the state in this light is really possible only for Christians. For only the Christian (and not many Christians at that) can combine forgiveness (not holding the other's sins against him), with repentance (the

78

willingness to see one's own sin). The pagan sees all the sin on the "other side" and the proclamation of repentance is therefore the only liberation from selfishness and the only basis of objectivity. [10]

Second, the message of the prophets always took a negative form. In spite of all the ammunition which the social gospel theology took from the Old Testament prophets, those prophets do not propose a detailed plan for the administration of society. This is necessary in the nature of the case, for the state is not an ideal order, ideally definable; it is a pragmatic tolerable balance of egoisms and can become more or less tolerable. To define the point of infinite tolerability would be to define the kingdom; it can not be done in terms of the present situation. Thus the prophet, or the prophetic church, speaks first of all God's condemnation of concrete injustices; if those injustices are corrected, new ones may be tackled. Progress in tolerability may be achieved, as the democracies of Switzerland, England, and the Netherlands show us; but only in limited degree and in specific areas, and the means of progressing is not defining of utopias but the denouncing of particular evils and the invention of particular remedies. On the larger perspective the forces of disintegration are advancing as rapidly as the church. We need not to be embarrassed when the politician asks us what he should do; our first answer is that he is already not doing the best that he knows, and he should first stop the injustice he is now committing and implement the ideals he now proclaims.

The relation of this entire development to an understanding of nonresistant Christian pacifism is obvious. It is just as clear that the New Testament, by its ethics as well as by its eschatology, rejects most kinds of nationalism, militarism, and vengeance for the Christian and calls him to return good for evil. Any attempt to draw from Scriptures an approval of war in principle, on the basis of what John the Baptist said to soldiers, what Jesus said before Gethsemane, what Samuel said to Saul, or of Jesus' use of a whip when He cleansed the temple, is condemned to failure.

We must, however, give greater respect to the one serious argument which remains to justify participation in war. This argument has not always been clearly distinguished from the untenable exegetical points just mentioned; but it has another foundation, and in its purest form it admits that nonresistance is God's will for the Christian, and that war is evil. In spite of this concession it is held that in a social situation where third parties are involved nonresistance is not the full response to the problem of evil. The Christian as an individual should turn the other cheek; but in society he has a responsibility for the protection of his good neighbors against his bad neighbors — in short, what we have seen to be the police function of the state. This is not to say that the good neighbors are wholly good or the bad wholly bad; but in the conflict in question, one neighbor's egoism coincides more closely with order and justice than the other's. It is therefore the Christian's duty, through the functions of the state, to contribute to the maintenance of order and justice in this way. Even war as an extreme case may be justified, when the alternative would be permitting passively the extension of tyranny which is worse than war.

We must recognize the sincerity and the consistency of this viewpoint, and the honest realism which its proponents demonstrate when they do not claim to be angels or to have a divine mission to go crusading. This view of the function of the state is the only true and reliable one, and coincides with the biblical view of the police function of the state under the lordship first of Jahweh, then of Christ. That is precisely our objection to it; this view, based on a realistic analysis of the old aeon, knows nothing of the new. It is not specifically Christian, and would fit into any honest system of social morality. If Christ had never become incarnate, died, risen, ascended to heaven, and sent His Spirit, this view would be just as possible, though its particularly clear and objective expression results partly from certain Christian insights.

The contemporary slogan which expresses this prevalent attitude to war and other questions of a social nature, especially in contemporary ecumenical and neo-orthodox or "chastened-liberal" circles, is the term "responsibility." This term is extremely dangerous, not because of what it says, but because of its begging the question and its ambiguity. The question which matters is not whether this Christian has a responsibility for the social order, it is *what* that responsibility is. Those who use this slogan, however, proceed from the affirmation that there is *a* responsibility to the conclusion (contained in *their* definition of responsibility) that it must be expressed in a specific way, including the ultimate possibility of war.[11] The error here is not in the affirmation that there is a real Christian responsibility to the social order; it is rather in the (generally unexamined and unavowed) presuppositions which result in that responsibility's being defined from within the given order alone rather than from the gospel as it infringes upon the situation. Thus the sinful situation itself becomes the norm, and there can be no such thing as Christian ethics derived from revelation.

We have seen that there is a real responsibility of the Christian to the social order but that, to be accurate, it must distinguish between the objects of its witness. Thus we find the basic error of the "responsible" position to be its Constantinian point of departure. This starting point leads first of all to confusion as to the *agent* of Christian ethics. Since the distinction between church and world is largely lost, the "responsible" church will try to preach a kind of ethics which will work for non-Christians as well as Christians. Or, better said, since everyone in such a society may consider himself Christian, the church will teach ethics not for those who possess the power of the Holy Spirit and an enabling hope but for those whose Christianity is conformity. This excludes at the outset any possibility of putting Christian ethics in its true light and concludes by making consistent Christianity the "prophetic calling" of a few, who may be useful if only they don't claim to be right.

But the most serious criticism of this definition of social concern is its preference of the old aeon to the new, and the identification of the church's mission and the meaning of history with the function of the state in organizing sinful society. This preference is so deeply anchored and so unquestioned that it seems scandalously irresponsible of the "sectarians" to dare to question it. This is why the American churches as a whole are embarrassed to be asked to talk of eschatology. Yet it is clear in the New Testament that the meaning of history is not what the state will achieve in the way of a progressively more tolerable ordering of society, but what the church achieves through evangelism and through the leavening process. This "messianic self-consciousness" on the part of the church looks most offensive to the proponents of a modern world view, but it is what we find in the Bible.

The claim is frequent that by not taking over himself the police function in society the Christian would abandon this function to evil men or to the "demonic." Again, this apparently logical argument is neither quite biblical nor quite realistic: (a) because the police function would be abandoned not to the demonic but to the reign of Christ; (b) because through the "leavening" process, Christianized morality seeps into the non-Christian mind through example and through the education of children who do not themselves choose radical Christianity, with the result that the whole moral tone of non-Christian society is changed for the better and there are honorable and honest men available to run the government before the church is numerically strong enough for "responsibility" to be a meaningful concept. (A case in point: Quakerism, Methodism, and the revivals along the American frontier did more to give a moral tone to Anglo-Saxon democratic traditions than did Anglican and Puritan politicking — once again, leavening works better than policing); (c) because the prophetic function of the church, properly interpreted, is more effective against injustice than getting into the political machinery oneself; (d) because there always exists the potential corrective power of other egoisms (Assyria in Is. 10) to keep any abuse from going too far.

It is within the scope of this "responsibility" mentality that the argument of the "lesser evil" is formulated. While it shows commendable honesty in refusing to claim that violence and war are good, it betrays still more logical confusion in the use of the terms. Generally neither the agent, the nature of evil, the criteria for comparing evils, nor the relation of means to ends is clearly defined, much less biblically derived.

Leaving aside several valid criticisms at this point, let us give the "lesser evil" argument its most defensible form. The contention is that out of love for my Neighbor A I should protect him when Neighbor B attacks him, for if I did not I should share the guilt for the attack. Being guilty of defensive violence against Neighbor B is less evil than being passively guilty of permitting offensive violence against Neighbor A for one of two reasons: either because Neighbor B is the aggressor or because Neighbor A is my friend or relative or fellow citizen for whom I have more responsibility than for Neighbor B.

The nonresistant answer here cannot help being scandalous and pushing the scandal of the cross to the end. If the cross defines *agape*, it denies:

    a. that "one's own" family, friends, compatriots, are more to be loved than the enemy;[12]

b. that the life of the aggressor is worth less than that of the attacked;

c. that the responsibility to prevent evil (policing Neighbor B) is an expression of love (it is love in the sense of a benevolent sentiment but not of *agape* as defined by the cross) when it involves the death of the aggressor;

d. that letting evil happen is as blameworthy as committing it.

These four denials are implicit in the positive development of this treatment. To develop them further here would be repetition. That these denials appear scandalous demonstrates simply how thoroughly the western Christian mind-set has been Constantinianized, i.e., influenced by pagan and pre-Christian ideas of particular human solidarities as ethical absolutes.

When this argument is phrased in terms of the war question, its customary formulation is the claim that tyranny is worse than war. Apart from the confusion of agents (tyranny is the tyrant's fault, war would be ours), this raises seriously the question of ends and means. For "absolutist" ethics ends and means are inseparable and there can be no legitimate calculation of predictable success. For "lesser evil" ethics, however, the comparison of results is paramount and, once mystical arguments about fighting on to the death against all odds are rejected (on the lesser-evil basis), it is hard to demonstrate that the national autonomy, even with the cultural values it protects, would be a greater loss than what would be destroyed in an atomic-bacterial-chemical war and in the totalitarization even of the "free" nations which war now involves. Since no one but Gandhi has tried submission to tyranny, the comparison is hard to make; but the nations which in World

War II resisted Hitler the most violently did not necessarily suffer the least thereby. For the Christian disciple, it is clear from Jesus' attitude to the Roman occupation forces and His rejection of the Zealots' aims and methods, as well as from the first centuries of Christian history, that war is not preferable to tyranny; i.e., that the intention of liberating one's people from despotic rule does not authorize the use of unloving methods. In fact the claim that God is especially interested in any people's political autonomy or that God has charged any one modern nation with a particular mission which makes its survival a good *in ipso* is precisely what is pagan about modern particularized Constantinianism. Personal survival is for the Christian not an end in itself; how much less national survival.

A second objection to the "lesser-evil" argument is the incapacity of man to calculate the results of his action in such a way as to measure hypothetical evils one against another, especially to measure the evil he would commit against the evil he would prevent. The very decision to base one's ethical decisions on one's own calculations is in itself already the sacrifice of ethics to opportunism. Such calculations are highly uncertain, due to the limits of human knowledge and to the distortion of objective truth by man's pride. To shift our critique to the Christian plane: the way in which God works in history has often been such as to confound the predictions of the pious and the faithful, especially those who tied their predictions about God's working too closely to their national welfare. The most significant contributions to history have in the past often been made not by the social strategists, who from a position of power sought to steer toward the lesser predictable evil, but by the "sectarians" whose eschatological consciousness made it sensible for them to act in apparently irresponsible ways. The most effective way to contribute to the preservation of society in the old aeon is to live in the new.

A third objection, which should be of basic significance to the "responsible" school even though notice is seldom taken of it, is that the effect of the "lesser evil" argument in historical reality is the opposite of its intent. Consistently applied, this argument would condemn most wars and most causes for war, and would permit a war only as a very last resort, subject to strictly defined limitations; yet the actual effect of this argument upon the church's witness is to authorize at least the war for which the nation is just now preparing, since at least *this* war is a very last resort. Whereas in intent this position should hold wars within bounds and would condemn at any rate the wars now being waged and being prepared, its effect on those who hear theologians speaking thus is to make war or the threat of war a first resort. Whereas in consistent application the "lesser-evil" argument would lead in our day to a pragmatic (though not absolutist) pacifism and to the advocacy of nonviolent means of resistance, in reality it authorizes the church to accept the domination of modern society by militarism without effective dissent.

This writer was present in 1950-51 when Karl Barth dealt with war and related questions in the lectures which were to become volume III/4 of his *Church Dogmatics*. For most of an hour his argument was categorical, condemning practically all the concrete causes for which wars have been and may be fought. The students became more and more uneasy, especially when he said that pacifism is "almost infinitely right." Then came the dialectical twist, with the idea of a divine vocation of self-defense assigned to a particular nation, and a war which Switzerland might fight was declared — hypothetically admissible. First there was a general release of tension in a mood of "didn't think he'd make it," then applause. What is significant here is the difference between what Barth said and what the students understood. Even though a consistent application of Karl Barth's teaching would condemn *all wars* except those fought to defend the independence of small Christian republics, and even though Barth himself now takes a position categorically opposed to nuclear weapons, calling himself in fact "practically pacifist,"[13] every half-informed Christian thinks Karl Barth is not opposed to war. Similarly, Reinhold Niebuhr's justification of American military preparedness is used by the Luce thinking of some American patriots to justify a far more intransigent militarism than Niebuhr himself could accept. This tendency of theologians' statements to be misinterpreted is also part of "political reality." Even the most clairvoyant and realistic analysis of the modern theologian is thus powerless against the momentum of the Constantinian compromise. Once the nation is authorized *exceptionally* to be the agent of God's wrath, the heritage of paganism makes quick work of generalizing that authorization into a divine rubber stamp.

Footnotes

1. The Second General Assembly of the World Council of Churches, planned for summer 1954 in Evanston, Illinois, under the topic, "Christ, the Hope of the World," set the theme of the Heerenwegen conference.

2. This particular list of major affirmations is that of C. H. Dodd, in his *The Apostolic Preaching and Its Developments*, Willett, Clark and Company, 1937, esp. pp. 9-15.

3. This paragraph uses the word "political" to designate the structures of the human community "under the sign of the old aeon," which was the predominant usage in theological conversation at the time. The rest of this book is committed to a more contemporary and more helpful usage, in which the work and will of Christ should be spoken of as "political" in the most proper sense of this term, i.e., as having to do with the *polis*, the common life of men. While the writer strongly prefers his contemporary usage, the difference between what is said in the rest of this book by accepting the characterization "political" and what is said in the above (1954) passage by rejecting the word differ only semantically.

4. Peter's sermon at Pentecost, Acts 2:17, interprets Pentecost as the fulfillment of Joel 2:28.

5. Hebrews 8:8-12 characterizes the new covenant as the fulfillment of this promise from Jeremiah 31:33.

6. Compare our fuller treatment of the theme of sharing in the suffering of Christ in *The Politics of Jesus*, Chap. VIII.

7. The phrase "replacing disobedient Israel" should not be understood as attributing to the N.T. writers the anti-Semitism of the second Christian century. The disobedience of Israel was a constantly recurring theme of the Hebrew prophets. The testimony of the apostles is not that Israel is displaced but rather that Israel is restored or rediscovered in a new form which takes Gentiles into the covenant.

8. Oscar Cullmann, *The State in the New Testament*, Scribners, 1956.

9. The Heerenwegen conference at which this paper was first presented was immediately followed by a working session of the Continuation Committee of the Historic Peace Churches and the International Fellowship of Reconciliation, which completed the editorial work for the text, "Peace Is the Will of God," which was then jointly submitted by them to the World Council of Churches just prior to the Evanston assembly. "Peace Is the Will of God" has again been reprinted in the collection of documents from the ecumenical conversation, *The Christian and War*, Historic Peace Churches and International Fellowship of Reconciliation, London, Paris, and Scottdale, 1970.

10. "The Christian" in this paragraph refers to a stance and a state of mind. The "pagan" describes not particular adherents of other religions, but rather the personal stance and state of mind from which the Christian confesses himself to have been freed. Cf. Andre Trocme, *The Politics of Repentance*, and Herbert Butterfield, *Christianity, Diplomacy, and War*,

.Abingdon-Cokesbury, 1953, "Human Nature and Human Culpability," pp. 41 ff.

11. The precise argumentative meaning which the word "responsible" has come to have in Protestant political ethical discussion is further analyzed in a later chapter, "Christ the Light of the World," esp. p. 142.

12. The preference for the enemy over the friend as an object of the Christian's moral responsibility is explicitly stated in Matthew 5 and Luke 6. It is founded in the nature of the love of God, who favors His enemies in loving rebellious men and seeking their restoration.

13. Karl Barth, *Church Dogmatics* IV/2, T & T Clark, 1958, p. 550. The original German makes the point even more clearly against the interpretation his position is polularly given, *Die Kirchliche Dogmatik* IV/2, Evangelischer Verlag, 1955, p. 622.

IV. IF ABRAHAM IS OUR FATHER*

One basic problem of interpretation, which cannot be avoided by Christians whose commitment to nonresistance or pacifism is oriented around loyalty to Jesus Christ, is the issue of the Old Testament. The entire impression left with the modern reader by the narrative of the Hebrew Bible is one of violence being not merely tolerated but fostered and glorified. This impression seems to be present throughout the Old Testament, and to constitute a logical unity. It is visible especially in the following forms:

    a. The holy warfare of the age of Moses, Joshua, and the judges.

    b. The civil legislation of the Pentateuch, with its provision for the death penalty, and other kinds of retaliation, short of death, which seem to breathe a spirit other than that of forgiveness.

    c. The importance of the national existence of the kingdoms of Israel and Judah, the narrative of which turns

---

*Drawn from class lectures in a course on Christian attitudes to war, peace, and revolution taught at Associated Mennonite Biblical Seminaries in 1968-69 and at the University of Notre Dame in 1969-70.

so largely about the fate and fortune of the kingly house.

   d. The imprecatory Psalms and prophetic visions which rejoice at the prospect of the destruction of the enemies of Israel.

Let it be noted before we proceed in an effort to analyze more fully this problem, that it constitutes a problem only if one is committed to a particular understanding of Jesus, His work, and His way. Thus all those whose positions are to be described in the following outline (and which we may criticize for certain inadequacies) must first of all be recognized as standing within a commonality of prior commitment. The problem being faced here arises only if one *is* agreed that the demand of the New Testament is for nonresistance.

In the face of this problem there seem to be only a certain number of possible explanations. They recur all through the centuries.

A. The New Dispensation

The Sermon on the Mount, in which we find the most concentrated statement of the ethical demand of Jesus, repeats six times the formula, "You have learned that our forefathers were told. . . . But what I tell you is this. . . ." It has seemed self-evident to many that Jesus here is announcing the beginning of a new era or dispensation which purely and simply sets aside what went before. There need therefore be no embarrassment about the contradiction with the sacred writings of old; Jesus takes it upon Himself to declare them no longer binding. Thus in Peter of Cheltchitz in

92

some early Anabaptists and Quakers, in Tolstoy and numerous modern Protestants, the sweeping novelty of the new covenant is a total answer to this problem.

This conception of a newly instituted dispensation is compatible with many modern theological leanings toward a progressive or evolutionary idea of religious truth. It is, however, also quite compatible with a very conservative conception of the sovereignty of God, within whose privileges it must always belong to change His orders, to establish a new basis upon which men are to live, without being accountable to anyone for seeming inconsistency or contradiction.[1] Thus the very conservative school of Protestantism known as "dispensationalism" sees not two but several, often as many as seven, different schemes whereby God has chosen to regulate His relationship to His people. The movement from one dispensation to the next is the forward movement of history. Since God is purposeful in making each move, it would be the height of impudence for men to try to discern in that movement any contradiction.

This "dispensational" interpretation has therefore had a great attraction for especially the more rigorous and systematic minds among Christian pacifists. Yet it has some serious shortcomings.

1. Jesus does not say He is setting aside the Old Testament. None of the texts which He "sets aside" is a quotation from the Old Testament. They rather represent misinterpretations or abuses of the original intent of the Old Testament demand. In some of the cases He specifically sharpens or clarifies the intent of the earlier saying and does not find fault with it at all. He prefaces this series of six "But I say to you" passages with the claim that He is

about to demand a righteousness greater than that of the scribes and Pharisees and a fulfillment of even the smallest letter of the law, which He does not come to abolish. It thus seems to do serious violence to the context of the Sermon on the Mount to see in it any conscious setting aside of the Old Testament law.[2]

2. To be certain, with the kind of logical rigor which ought to apply when talking about the abolition of a legal code, one would need to be quite clear as to just when the abolition of the old has been declared and by just what authority. Is the whole Old Testament done away with or just a particular legal requirement? If it is just certain segments which are done away with, how are we to determine what they are and what is still valid? Can we really believe it to be a part of the faith of the Jew Jesus that nothing would be left of the authority of His people's Bible? But then if not everything is done away with we need a very careful procedure for determining what it is that remains. Such a careful procedure is not self-evident, nor is it provided with any clarity by the dispensationalist theologies. Some of them, as a matter of fact, do not find a clear command for nonresistance in the New Testament, since they assign the Sermon on the Mount to a different age from that in which the church now lives. It is all very well to appeal to the unaccountable sovereignty with which God has arrived to prescribe a law to His creatures and to change that law; but it is quite another matter for the creature to make such distinctions and to attribute changed purposes to God when He has not clearly said so.

Thus both the claim of Jesus to represent the claim of fulfillment of Israelite faith and Jewish hope, and the claim of the God of the Bible to be a faithful and reliable witness are seriously jeopardized by a sweeping shift of dispensations, unless we are to be provided with some far more clear way of measuring the why and the wherefore of the shift, its extent and its char-

94

acter. On the face of the text, the words of Jesus in Matthew 5 do not suffice to sweep away our problem, for to do so would demand that they sweep away the entire Old Testament, which is clearly not their intent.

B. A Shift of Degree; Concession to Disobedience

It is possible to interpret Jesus' words, "But I say," not as a fundamental shift of the divine purpose but as pointing to a new stage in its definition and realization. We could say that the purpose of God has always been the same, but that He made a permissive concession to the unwillingness or unreadiness of men to accept or to obey His full intent.[3] There is a shift from old to new, but that shift is the termination or the withdrawal of the concession.

The strongest support for this interpretation is the text of Matthew 19 with regard to the provision of Deuteronomy 24 for divorce. "It was because your minds were closed that Moses permitted you to divorce your wives; but it was not like that when all began" (Mt. 19:8). Now that Jesus has restored the wholeness of the knowledge of God's creative purposes, or the possibility of obeying Him, the concession to men's hard hearts or closed minds is withdrawn.

This position has certain logical advantages over the preceding one. In addition, it recognizes a real shift, a real change in God's prescriptions, but it does not leave this shift unaccountably to be blamed on an arbitrary divine decision or an inscrutable change of divine purposes. Man, not God, is responsible for the concession. It was an attribute of God's patience that He made such a concession, but it never was really His will.

The difficulty of this approach is that it would be very difficult to demonstrate any common measure between the place which war and national sentiment on the one hand and the possibility of divorce on the other have in the Old Testament or the significance of nonresistant love on one hand and the permanence of marriage on the other in the New Testament. If there be a parallel of logic, it is at least striking that the concept of the divine concession is made so clear with regard to divorce, an ethical issue where the contrast is not enormous and about which both testaments say relatively little, but that it never comes to the surface with regard to war, a contrast which is greater and an issue which is far more widely represented.

Nor does this approach quite fit the shape of the Old Testament material. Divorce is never commanded in the Old Testament; it is only grudgingly permitted, and that in a context whose main intent is to restrain it and to protect the dignity of woman. Thus even this legislation in its very words supports the theme of "concession." This *cannot* be said about a holy war. It can be said about some of the narrative with regard to Israelite national identity and specifically the adoption of the institution of royalty, concerning which the narrators and the prophets' evaluations are ambivalent. But both in the death penalty and in the imperative to holy war, the concept of concession is certainly foreign to the material.

C. The Pedagogical Concession

Perhaps God was making an adjustment not to a culpable hardness of heart but to an innocent primitive moral immaturity. Perhaps insight into the destructiveness of violence and the redemptiveness of love is a very refined kind of cultural understanding accessible only to cultures with a certain degree of advancement. It would have been too much to ask for the rough and illiterate tribesmen of the age of Moses and Joshua. For the age of Jesus, however, standing on the shoulders of the civilizing preparation of later prophets and the experience of exile and Roman rule, the nature of such an imperative became much more readily conceivable.

This conception of the pedagogical concession can perhaps be compared to the difference between a parent's commanding a child not to touch matches or electric plugs at the age of two and his instructing the child to use matches or an electric plug a few years later. The parent is not inconsistent, nor has the nature of fire or electricity changed; but there have been changes in the capacity of the child to understand and to use them. Actions may be permissible or even mandatory when he understands how to do them which were forbidden and harmful before.

One difficulty with this kind of position is its traditional correlation with an evolutionist liberal theological perspective. To hold a view like this one must look down on the ancient Israelites with a sense of moral superiority which is difficult to justify on objective grounds. One must also take a rather cavalier

attitude toward the authority of the scriptural narratives, which affirm explicit and affirmative divine instructions hardly able to be subsumed under the heading of "adjustment to immaturity." It could be pointed
out also that the analogy of the child's use of fire is
significantly reversed. In the case of Israelite warfare
it is the command which comes early and the prohibition late. The same conception of the growing capacity
to act with insight would not seem to fit as well in
this case.

D. The Division of Levels or Realms

In view of the shortcomings of each of these views
which seeks to interpret Old Testament warfare as
somehow less binding or exemplary than New Testament nonresistance, it is no surprise that the main
stream of Christian interpretation has resolved the
question by dividing the materials into different levels.
One has no difficulty in reconciling the Old Testament
and the New if one notices they are simply talking on
different subjects. One can affirm that the Bible is a
total unity, with all of its truths and instructions timelessly valid, and find no contradiction; it suffices to dis-
criminate one type of subject matter from another.

In the Old Testament we have narrative and imperative dealing with the civil life of the Hebrew people.
The commands and permissions which enabled that civil
order to defend itself, including the use of violence both
against social offenders and against enemies, were not
only legitimate for them but continue to give legitimacy
to the use of the death penalty and military violence by

98

the state in our age. The New Testament does not deny or retract any of this; it cannot since it is not on that subject. Nothing in the New Testament prescribes any standards for the civil order. The only New Testament texts which speak to that issue are those which recognize the civil order as being master in its own house. ("Render to Caesar that which is Caesar's," "Be subject to the powers that be"). The nonviolence, the renunciation of rights, and the willingness to suffer which are typical of the ethic of the New Testament are only imperatives for the Christian individual and apply only in his primary relationships or in the church. Thus there is no contradiction.

This approach has the great advantage of not really needing to solve the problem we have been working at. It merely sets it aside. It does have, however, some significant theological and logical shortcomings. One finds them when one attempts to neatly draw the line (which it takes for granted) between the individual and the social, or when one recognizes that the New Testament says far more about social and political orders than simply to command submission to Caesar. There is a further flaw in the clarity of definition when one asks just what it is in the civil prescriptions of the Old Testament that is supposed to be normative for the modern civil order. Does this include specific details such as the massacring of a city in a holy war, or the death penalty by stoning for a young man who talks back to his parents? Or is it only in some sense the general principle of civil order? If it is not only that, how do we draw the line between the principle and the specifics? The other fundamental weakness of this approach is that, in a way which is just the reverse of the weakness of the other dualistic positions, it seems able to recognize no movement at all in the course of holy history. Yet according to its own testimony this history is a matter of promise and fulfillment, or prediction and expectancy, and then of the coming of change.

E. The Concrete Historical Anthropological Meaning

All of the above views (except the dispensational shift), begin to state the problem by looking *back* upon the Old Testament from the New. Assuming in other words that God is always timelessly the same, and that He is ultimately the most clearly revealed in Jesus, how can He consistently, having always been the same, have willed something else in an earlier time? It is this assumed identity of the divine will over time which creates the problem. But the story did not move that way, back over the Old Testament from the perspective of the New; it was rather a purposeful movement in the other direction.

If we look at the Old Testament from the perspective of the New we are struck by the difference, and the difference seems to lie at the point of whether killing is forbidden or not. But if we were instead to look at the events of the old story as they happened, moving toward the new, we should have been struck by quite another kind of consideration. It is therefore more proper, in reading the Old Testament story, to ask not how it is different from what came later, but rather how it differs from what went *before* or what prevailed at the time, and how it moves toward what was to come later. If we put the question in this way, we then find that the diversity of imperatives regarding killing is not the basic issue. What is most fundamentally at stake is rather an understanding of the covenant community and its relationship to God who has called it and promised it His care.

Let us begin the exposition of a different approach with the command addressed to Abraham (Gen. 22) to sacrifice his son Isaac. This passage is consistently and systematically misinterpreted in Western ethical thought because it is measured from the present rather than from the context of the command. We know that for a man to kill his son, especially to sacrifice his son in a bloody ritual, is morally and culturally abhorrent. Thus the question for us as we interpret the story is how a man can deal with a command to do something which is thus abhorrent, and what it says about the absolute sovereignty of God that He reserves the right to command us to do such things.

But for Abraham in his culture there was nothing morally or culturally abhorrent about sacrificing the life of his firstborn. All the neighbors did the same thing. It was as natural to sacrifice one's firstborn son, because of the prior claim of God on the fertility of one's wife and as a way of assuring her future fertility, as it was to sacrifice the firstfruits of the field and the flock for the same reason. Fertility is after all a gift of God, and the firstfruits of the womb, just as of the flock and the fig tree, belong to Him. We thus misunderstand the Abraham story completely if we try to see in it the paradoxical command of a God telling a man to do something awful.

The other modern misunderstanding is to build in a parallel way upon the emotional attachment of a man to his child. Modern Western personalism has equipped us for a deep sentimental attachment of the father to the son; so that for a modern father to take the life of his son, in any state of mind except a drunken rage, is unthinkable. Thus we ask traditionally what it is supposed to tell us about the awfulness or the sovereignty or the paradoxical character of God that He would ask man to do something so contrary to his deepest nature and drives. But again we modernize. This kind of sentimental attachment of father to son, if it existed at all in the patriarchal age, can hardly have been viscerally as powerful as it is for us.

(By challenging these interpretations of the command to Abraham, we also challenge the Protestant sermonizing à la Kierkegaard or à la Bonhoeffer which have tried to make of this ancient story a proof that God is sovereignly unaccountable, or irrationally self-contradictory, or that His power is most clearly seen where our good sense and our sensitivity are summoned to bow blindly before Him.)

What then was the test put to Abraham? Why was it that it was a testing of his obedience to be ready to sacrifice his son, if the test was not to his ethics or to his fatherly sentiments? The wider story itself makes clear, as does the analysis of Hebrews (ch. 11), that the issue for Abraham was whether to trust his God for his survival. Isaac was his only legitimate son, and God had promised that Abraham would have a great posterity. How then could Abraham have posterity if his son were killed? Thus it was the promise of God Him-self, the achievement of God's proclaimed purposes, and not simply the tastes or the interests of Abraham, which were at stake. The question was not "can I sacrifice my interest to God?" but rather, "Can I obey God when He seems to be willing to jeopardize His own purposes?" The answer, "God will provide," is thus a reassurance not of our own survival or com-fort, but of the rationality of obedience which seems ready to jeopardize God's own purposes.[4]

Perhaps this exercise in questioning our cultural narrowness as we read the Bible may prepare us for a more flexible interpretation as we turn from it to the phenomenon of holy war in ancient Israel. Here we may follow broadly the pioneering study of Gerhard von Rad, followed by more detailed but largely unpublished studies of Millard Lind.[5]

What kind of social phenomenon was holy war in an-cient Israel? We should ask, we have said, not how it differed from New Testament discipleship but how it was original in its own cultural context.

In summary: what have been the main lines of this effort to interpret the Abraham story in its context? (a) We have sought to ward off any hasty interpreta-tions which come from asking ourselves what the very same command would mean for us; (b) we have sought to interpret the affirmative meaning in terms of the cultural options of the time and place of the account; (c) we have then sought for a way to formulate that element in Abraham's decision which is "translatable"; (d) in doing so we have taken our cue from the New Testament use of the same account. When interpreting the material in this way we have found that the issue of whether killing is right or wrong is simply not the issue with which to begin, if we wish our interpretation to be fair to the kind of story we are working with.

With this orientation let us now move back specifically to the religious warfare of the early Old Testament story. We have here to do with elements which are present throughout the narrative from the Red Sea to Saul. Recent scholarly work has analyzed these reports with considerable thoroughness.

We first observe that the issue of the rightness or wrongness of taking of life does not arise in these accounts. There is no discussion within them of any effort to relate these words to the teaching of the Decalogue which forbids killing. It is not argued that killing is wrong except in these circumstances (the lines of the later doctrine of the just war which was taken over from pagan philosophical tradition). The possibility had not yet come into view that the prohibition of killing in the Decalogue (as it was understood) would need somehow to be related to these wars.

The holy war of ancient Israel is a religious or a ritual event. Prominence is given in many of the accounts to the term *herem*, meaning "set apart" or *tabu*; before being attacked, a Canaanite city would be "devoted to Jahweh," a ceremony which made of that entire city, including its living inhabitants, a sacrificial object. The bloodshed which followed the victory was not conceived as the taking of the individual lives of persons, each of whom could be thought of as a father or a mother or a child; it was rather a vast, bloody sacrifice to the God who had "given the enemy into our hands." The enemy has been put to death not because he has been conceived of personally as an object of hate but because in a much more ritual way he becomes a human sacrifice.

This ritual context has in turn an economic side effect. If all the slaves and the flocks of the enemy are to be slaughtered in one vast sacrifice, there will then be no booty. The war does not become a source of immediate enrichment through plunder nor a source of squabbling among the soldiers about how to divide the spoils; for there are no spoils.

The holy war is not a result of strategic planning but an *ad hoc* charismatic event. Israel is under the pressure of a neighboring tribe; a leader arises who is not a part of any royal dynasty or professional military class, and in response to his call the men of Israel arrive bringing their own weapons, whatever tools (axes, hoes) they had just been using. There is no professional army and no military strategist. If Israel's forces win it is not because they were more expert or more numerous but because of a miracle: "Yahweh gave the enemy into their hands." Sometimes, especially as in the parade around Jericho and the wars of Gideon, special symbolic measures are taken to dramatize the non-rational, nonprofessional, miraculous character of the entire sacramental battle. When the Israelites want to have a king like other kings and a standing army like other nations have, *the holy wars come to an end.*

What the original experience of the holy wars meant in the life of Israel was that even at the very crucial point of the bare existence of Israel as a people, their survival could be entrusted to the care of Yahweh as their King, even if He told them to have no other kings. They did not need to trust to their own institutional readiness or the solidarity of their royal house; Jahweh would provide.

This interpretation of the central permanent meaning of the holy war story is supported by the appeal which is made to the holy war tradition by the later prophets and by the writer of the Book of Chronicles. These later interpreters do not derive from the tradition the conclusion, "Israel slaughtered the Amalekites and therefore we should put to death all the enemies of God." The point made by the prophets is rather, "Jahweh has always taken care of us in the past; should we not be able to trust His providence for the immediate future?" Its impact in those later prophetic proclamations was to work *against* the development of a military caste, military alliances, and political designs based on the availability of military power.

According to von Rad, a critical analysis of the narratives dealing with just war would indicate that the picture given by a superficial reading of the Book of Joshua is misleading in the idea it gives of a rapid military sweep across Palestine within a very limited period, and the consequent understanding of these military operations as aggressive and strategically concerted.[6] It seems more likely, according to the critical historical reconstruction, that the Israelites gradually infiltrated in the interstices between the Canaanite settlements, gradually becoming more settled and less nomadic, and then that they were threatened by the backlash of repressive efforts on the part of the earlier inhabitants.

The image given by the present text of the Book of Joshua is belied by the reports of Canaanite cities which persisted in the midst of Israel for generations and by the continuing reported presence within the same territory of Philistines, Canaanites, Ammonites, and other very close neighbors. Thus although the infiltration of the Israelites into Palestine had about it a certain aggressive character, the actual holy war military operations tended to be defensive.[7]

The Case for the Historical View

From this perspective we can avoid both the condescending and arbitrary approach of saying that the ancient Hebrews only thought that God told them to fight, and the concept of a "concession" in response to conscious disobedience. We can affirm that in these events there was, as the story says, a real word from the true Jahweh of hosts, speaking to His people in historically relevant terms.

The issue to which He spoke was not one of ethical generalizations and the limits of their validity. To place the question here is the source of our trouble. The issue to which this experience speaks is the readiness of God's people to be dependent upon miracles for survival. The holy war of Israel is the concrete experience of not needing any other crutches for one's identity and community as a people than trust in Jahweh as king, who makes it unnecessary to have earthly kings like the neighboring nations.

From the ancient Hebrews through the later prophets up to Jesus there was real historical movement, real "progress"; but the focus of this progress was not a changing of ethical codes but rather in an increasingly precise definition of the nature of peoplehood. The identification of the people of Israel with the state of Israel was progressively loosened by all of the events and prophecies of the Old Testament. It was loosened in a positive way by the development of an increasing vision for the concern of Yahweh for *all* peoples and by the promise of a time when *all* peoples would come to Jerusalem to learn the law; it was loosened as well in a negative direction by the development of a concept of the faithful remnant, no longer assuming that Israel as a geographical and ethnic body would be usable for Jahweh's purposes. These two changes in turn altered the relevance of the prohibition of killing. Once all men are seen as potential partakers of the covenant, then the outsider can no longer be perceived as less than human or as an object for sacrificing. Once one's own national existence is no longer seen as a guarantee of Jahweh's favor, then to save this national existence by a holy war is no longer a purpose for which miracles would be expected. Thus the dismantling of the applicability of the concept of the holy war takes place not by promulgation of a new ethical demand but by a restructuring of the Israelite perception of community under God.

Of the other viewpoints sketched earlier it is perhaps the concept of the pedagogical concession which is the more usable, but it still presupposes the kind of timeless understanding of "what God really wanted to get at," which undermines the genuinely historical nature of biblical faith. It also deceptively seems to locate the "fulness of time" in the outworking of God's purposes at the point of receptivity in the learner, rather than in the God-driven course of events themselves. The pedagogical concession gives us the picture of a curriculum through which each pupil can move at his own speed, and next year another set of pupils will work through the same curriculum again, the readiness of each pupil for the next learning being dependent upon how much he learned before. There is about salvation history a firmness and a definitiveness which does not fit with this picture of the repeatable curriculum. Jesus came only once in the fullness of time, because then His hour had come — not because a certain number of Jews had come to a point in their syllabus where they were ready for what He was next going to teach. The real working of a real God in real history is not to be reduced to progressing through a pre-digested curriculum at a certain rate determined by the capacity of the learner. It is not sure that men are any more "ready" or "mature" today than in Jesus' time, nor in Jesus' time than in Joshua's.

Thus, instead of being struck by a categorical difference between an Old Testament which permits killing and a New Testament which does not, we will observe positive movement along coherent lines, beginning with what is novel in holy war itself and moving in continuous steps to what is novel about the man Jesus. Already in the very first steps the note of dependence upon God for one's existence is new. Already in the very earliest legislation of early Israel there will be novelties, such as for instance the rejection of indirect retaliation which was a part of the contemporary laws of other peoples, and the greater dignity given to woman and the slave in Israelite legislation. Then progressively the prophetic line underlines these same dimensions as the story continues. Through the incorporation of persons of non-Israelite blood into the tribe, through the expansion of the world vision to include other nations, through the prophets' criticism of and history's destruction of kingship and territorial sovereignty as definitions of peoplehood, the movement continued through the centuries which was ultimately to culminate at the point where John the Baptist opened the door for Jesus.

"Do not claim that you are sons of Abraham; God can raise up sons of Abraham out of stones." To be the son of Abraham means to share the faith of Abraham. Thus the relativizing of the given ethnic-political peoplehood is completed in both directions. There is no one in any nation who is not a potential son of Abraham since that sonship is a miraculous gift which God can open up to Gentiles. On the other hand there is no given peoplehood which can defend itself against others as bearer of the Abrahamic covenant, since those who were born into that unity can and in fact already did jeopardize their claim to it by their unbelief. Thus the very willingness to trust God for the security and identity of one's peoplehood, which was the original concrete moral meaning of the sacrament of holy warfare, is now translated to become the willingness or readiness to renounce those definitions of one's own people and of the enemy which gave to the original sacrament its meaning.

Footnotes

1. This position is held, among others, by J. Irvin Lehman, *God and War*, Herald Press, 1942.

2. Jesus' relation to the OT is investigated in the first part of this study, "The Political Axioms of the Sermon on the Mount," especially pp. 34 ff.

3. Guy Hershberger *(War, Peace, and Nonresistance*, Herald Press, 1953) based his understanding of God's will with regards to killing on the "pedagogical adaptation." In this he was opposed by J. Irvin Lehman, *op. cit.*

4. If that were our subject the point would have to be made that this is the thrust of the entire passage of Hebrews 11:1 — 12:5. "Faith is the evidence of things not seen" (v. 1, AV) does not call for a blind willingness to swallow all kinds of improbable statements; the examples given by the rest of the passage make it clear that the meaning of the chapter is much more precise than that. Faith is what makes one willing to obey when it seems that obedience will not pay; when it seems that to obey is to jeopardize God's worthwhile purposes. "Faith" or "faithfulness" in this passage is therefore the attitude which makes obedience seem fitting in the face of odds.

5. Gerhard von Rad, *Der Heilige Krieg im Alten Israel*, Vandenhocck and Ruprecht, 1952. Millard C. Lind, "The Theology of Warfare in Ancient Israel," unpublished PhD dissertation, Western Theological Seminary, 1963. Millard C. Lind, "The Concept of Political Power in Ancient Israel" in *Annual of the Swedish Theological Institute* (Vol. VII), E. J. Brill, 1970, pp. 4-24.

6. von Rad, *op. cit,* pp. 14 ff.

7. Other studies have followed von Rad in exposing misconceptions held in relation to Israel's waging of war. However, their concern has been more to understand the problem in terms of the unmediated kingship of Jahweh over Israel. See my own argument, on subsequent pages, trying to work with the question of war as part of the question of God's kingship over Israel and His relation to other nations (pp. 105 ff.). Men like Lind *(op. cit.* and "Paradigm of Holy War in the Old Testament" an address to the Chicago Society of Biblical Research on its 80th anniversary, February 20, 1971) and P. D. Miller, Jr. ("Holy and Cosmic War in Early Israel," unpublished PhD dissertation, Harvard University, 1953) fault von Rad because he makes his claims concerning warfare in Israel on the basis of a radical questioning and reconstructing of the Joshua narratives. Taking a higher view of the biblical record, they see aggressive as well as defensive warfare as part of Israel's response to God. The kingship of Jahweh, however, gives warfare in ancient Israel a unique and limited character. There is critical and *textual* agreement that the Canaanites were still in the land generations later. Especially in light of other reports within Joshua and Judges, where the Canaanites are not completely swept out of the land, it is seen that an aggressive strategy, if present, was strictly limited.

ECUMENICAL PERSPECTIVES

I. LET THE CHURCH
BE THE CHURCH*

In the slogan, "Let the church be the church," which has been so sorely overworked in recent times, there is a paradox which is not only grammatical. The form of this call, "become what you are" is true to the New Testament pattern of thought. Especially the Apostle Paul, following a ringing proclamation of what it means to be a Christian, to be "in Christ," then frequently continues with an imperative, "let this be true of you." "Did you not die with Christ?" the apostle appeals, "Then put to death those parts of you which belong to the earth" (Col. 2:20; 3:5). After declaring that Christians have been made one (Eph. 2; 3), Paul continues with the appeal to them to act according to this call.

The call to "become what we are" means on the one hand that we are not being asked anything unnatural, anything impossible by definition. The summons is simply to live up to what a Christian — or the

---

*Rewritten from a lecture presented to the Episcopal Pacifist Fellowship at Seabury House, Greenwich, Connecticut, in August 1964. Previously published in *The Witness*, April 22, 1965, pp. 10 ff.

113

church — is when confessing that Christ is Lord.

And yet at the same time this imperative says negatively, "You are not what you claim to be." The church is not, fully and genuinely, all of what it means to be the church; otherwise we should not have to call her to become that reality which in Christ she is supposed to be. She has been giving her attention to being something other than the church. It is from this lack of clear dedication to her major cause that she needs to be called to cease trying to do something else and to become herself.

What then is the church and what should she be? One source will tell us that she is "one, holy, catholic, and apostolic;" another will tell us that she is to be found "where the sacraments are properly administered and the Word of God is properly preached." Still others would test her by the moral performance or the intensity of piety which can be seen in her individual members. But in our age there is arising with new clarity an understanding that what it means to be the church must be found in a clearer grasp of her relation to what is not the church, namely "the world." For us to say with the current ecumenical fashion that the church is a witnessing body, a serving body, and a body fellowshiping voluntarily and visibly, is to identify her thrice as not being the same thing as the total surrounding society. This definition demands for the church an existence, a structure, a sociology of her own, independent of the other structures of society. She can no longer be simply what "church" has so long meant in Europe, that administrative division of civil government which arranges to have preachers in the pulpits, nor can she be what is so often true in America, one more service club which, even though it has many members registered, still needs to compete with other loyalties for their time and attention.

One of the stimuli of the rediscovery of the significance of the church as a sociological reality has been the great foreign missionary movement of the past century. Missionaries have needed, if they were to preach outside the West, a different understanding of what is different about being a Christian than was needed in Europe's Middle Ages; for then to be a Christian was not to be different. Other developments have helped too. Within biblical studies there has been in recent decades a renewed awareness of the uniqueness of Israel's being a covenant people, and of the New Testament church's constituting a new kind of social reality. The ecumenical movement has begun to make Christians think of the church in other places around the world as a human reality to which they owe loyalty, warning them that simple identification with a local or national community and its religious authorities is not enough. Even in the "secular sciences" of psychology and sociology there are new developments which can enable us to see the reality of the church as a different kind of community more clearly than before.

In all of man's effort to understand his experience he has been prone to polarize. Christians have traditionally distinguished between the visible church and the invisible church, between the spirit and the body, between the ordained and the laity, between love and justice. We may now come to see that a more useful and a more biblical distinction would be one which does not try to distinguish between realms of reality like body and spirit or the visible and the invisible, nor between categories defined by ritual (lay and ordained), or by abstraction (love and justice), but rather between the basic personal postures of men, some of whom confess and others of whom do not confess that Jesus Christ is Lord. The distinction between church and the world is not something that God has imposed upon the world by a prior metaphysical definition, nor is it only something which timid or Pharisaical Christians have built up around themselves. It is all of that in creation that has taken the freedom not yet to believe.

In recent centuries those denominations whose heritage was that of the European state church have in many places moved significantly to modify or temper the effects of that relationship of mutual subservience between "church" and government. Yet there remains a far deeper job if we are to contemplate changing the categories of thought so as to deal not only with institutional relations but with the moral and psychological implications of that identification of church and society which stems from the age of Constantine.

The old yardsticks for knowing what constitutes a church used to be called the "marks" (notae) of the church. They pointed almost exclusively to characteristics which could be measured by looking right at the management of the church's liturgy or her business. They had to do with theological affirmations, with the qualification of clergy and the meaning of the sacraments. But today increasingly it is coming to be recognized that the real tests of whether the church is the church calls for measurements to be taken not in the meeting nor in the administrative structure but at the point of the relation of church and world. When Willem A. Visser 't Hooft wrote of *The pressure of our common calling,* [1] the three marks of the church in mission to which he pointed were all defined with reference to her distinct nature as church; not by the identification of the church with the total society but rather in her distinctness from it. The presuppositions of a relevant witness or ministry are a distinctiveness, a "having crossed over"; otherwise there is nothing to offer. Mission, then, is her witness to her distinctiveness, her calling, rather than to the church's own self-confidence.

When we confess that Christ is the light of the world this implies a critical attitude toward other pretended "lights." When we confess that Jesus Christ is Lord, this commits us to a relative independence of other loyalties which we would otherwise feel it normal to be governed by. [2] Likewise with reference to the nature of the church it must be said that the identification of the church with a given society, for which the church-state marriage of the Middle Ages was a sign and a safeguard, is wrong. This is not only because of the ultimate outworking in the religiously sanctioned national selfishness into which such Christians may fall, (and have fallen in the history of the West) but even in the prior idea that one given society could be somehow "Christianized" or "sanctified" through the church's possession of such authority in its midst.

It is especially from the Anglican tradition that the rest of us have learned something of the pervasive in-

117

tellectual power of the idea of Incarnation. It has been a most impressive vision, to say that all human concerns have been divinely sanctioned and hallowed by God's coming among us, taking on our flesh. Gardening and the weather, our work and our family, the total fabric of our society — economics and warfare, have been bathed in the light of God's presence. All of humanity is thus now seen to be good, wholesome, holy. This seems to a non-Episcopalian to be a deceptively incomplete way of saying something that is nonetheless deeply true. When God came among men He did nôt approve of and sanction *everything*, in "normal, healthy human society"; He did not make of *all* human activity, not even of all well-intentioned human activity, a means of grace. There are some loyalties and practices in human community which He rejected when He came among us. When God came among men He was born in a migrant family and not in a palace. Abraham the father of the faithful forsook the great civilization of Chaldea to become a nomad; Israel escaped from Egypt.

The pattern of faithfulness is one of genuine obedience in human experience — which we may well call Incarnation; but it is always also a break with the continuities of human civilization and the loyalties of local human societies, which we call Election or Exodus. When we then speak of Incarnation it must not mean God sanctifying our society and our vocations as they are, but rather His reaching into human reality to say what we must do and what we must leave behind. [3] Not all of life is to be blessed; not all human efforts can be penetrated by the glow of divine indwelling. In a world which is not yet the kingdom of Christ, it is through the initiative of the Incarnation that we can trace the reality of human obedience. Yet that obedience, at the same time that it is truly human, is also clearly different from the world around us. *God's pattern of Incarnation is that of Abraham, and not of Constantine.*

Permit me to clarify by caricature. The church in the past has been in this respect most properly represented by the chaplain. Whether in industry, in a university, in the military, or in the feudal prince's court from which the term is derived, the chaplain is called to bless an existing power structure. He is given this place by the authority in power; he is supported by that authority and in turn will put the stamp of divine approval upon what is being done there. His social posture is defined by his renouncing the liberty ultimately to challenge the selfish purposes of the community which he serves and for which he prays at the proper times. For him thus to stand in judgment upon this community would be first of all to condemn his own service to it, for his own ritual and moral support of that community's doing in the name of religion is itself the strongest claim the community makes to righteousness.

This "chaplaincy" stance in society can work out in one of two ways. If the preacher is a powerful person and the "prince" or general whom he serves is well-intentioned, the effort may be made to use the power of his position and that of his patron to impose upon all of society that vision of morality which is prescribed by religion. The chaplain has the ear of the prince and will use that power to oblige people to live the way they should according to his faith. This is the pattern we have come to describe as "puritan," and we all have some idea of what it does to the soul of a community. Those who do keep the rules are proud of it because they can; those who do not wish to keep them or cannot because of the way they are defined, are crushed or driven away. Furthermore since everyone is to be obliged to keep most of the rules, only those rules can be stated which can be enforced. You can forbid polygamy; you cannot prevent impure thoughts. Puritanism thus concentrates its attack upon the coarse and crude sins which it is possible externally to punish or prevent.

The alternative for the chaplain who does not wish to be Puritan, and who renounces the effort to use his position of power as a level to change society, will be to limit himself to calling down sacramentally the blessing of God upon society, sanctioning whatever means society (or rather the prince) needs to keep society (or rather the prince's place in it) afloat. Then the moral standards which he preaches will be those which are feasible for everyone. The understanding of God's purposes which guides his preaching will be that which is in line with the interests, the capacities, and the needs of his employer. He will say that it is proper, legitimate, to do all of those things which in his society seem to be necessary to preserve its prosperity and its authorities. In other ages this argument went under the heading of "the divine right of kings" or the "just war;" today one speaks of "responsibility."

This being our heritage, most debates about ethics

have been between the Puritans and the priests. It is between those who say that there are objective, absolute standards which must be forced on everyone, and those who say that if we have to do what we have to do we had better be able to say it is morally all right. This debate, although it is constantly being renewed with new vocabulary, is fruitless; for it defines the issues in such a way that a Christian solution is logically excluded. Both the Puritan and the priestly positions are looking for a course of human behavior which is possible, feasible, and accessible to all conditions of men; one which will "pay" in terms of survival and efficacy. The demands of ethics must be "possible" so that after having done whatever he did (as an effective Puritan or priest doing what is necessary) a man can say to himself that he is righteous because of what he did.

But Christian ethics calls for behavior which is impossible except by the miracles of the Holy Spirit. When we set up the question in such a way that the ethical prescriptions we hope to unfold must be within the realm of possibility, the cards must have been stacked against a Christian answer. This Puritan-priestly debate is furthermore fruitless because it is about form and not substance. It debates whether ethical standards are absolute or not, rather than asking what particular standards should be applied. The entire argument about how to be politically relevant can be run through at book length without any specific statements of value preference derived in a demonstrable way from the center of what the New Testament story is about.

If this insoluble controversy between the Puritan and the priest is the natural result of the position of the chaplain, then the solution to the problem can not be a new set of definitions of terms or a different set of Bible verses to quote. The solution must begin on the level of sociology, restoring the church to that posture in the world which is in accord with her message. It must renounce seeking a new doctrine for the court preacher to preach, which will leave him in his pulpit but make him either "more effective" or "more flexible" in prescribing a Christian morality for society as a whole, with special consideration for the strategic importance of the man at the top.

The alternative to Constantine was Abraham, father of the faithful. And what was the posture of Abraham? Or of Moses? That of the prophet who was listened to by only a minority. To recognize that the church is a minority is not a statistical but a theological observation. It means our convinced acceptance of the fact that we cannot oblige the world to hold the faith which is the basis of our obedience, and therefore should not expect of the world that kind of moral performance which would appropriately be the fruit of our faith. *Therefore* our vision of obedience cannot be tested by whether we can ask it of everyone.

By now, in the age of secularism, everyone is ready to recognize that we cannot oblige the world to be Christian. But is the recognition to be grudging or joyful? We grumpily abandon the vision of Christianizing the world by controlling it, because after having been tried for a millennium and a half this vision has broken down. Instead, should we not recognize repentantly that we ought never have wanted to Christianize the world in this way, from the top down, through the prestige of governmental backing and wide social acceptance? Now that the church has become weak may we not recognize with joy that her calling is to be weak? Should we not, by definition and without reluctance, renounce all grasping for the levers of control by which other people think they can govern history?

One of the logical implications of the acceptance of minority status will be that we no longer hold ourselves to be morally or psychologically obligated to tailor our moral standards to the needs of the people who are running the world. The most frequent response to the initial peace testimony of Christian pacifists is, "What would happen if everybody did this?" Since we are all children of Christendom we think we must answer this; but logically we need not and cannot — because everybody will not.

It was Immanuel Kant who gave the classic statement of this logic by saying, "I have the right to apply to myself only such standards as I could wish would be applied by everyone." As long as this principle is stated hypothetically it may still have some use. But Christian faith is possible only on the grounds of repentance and forgiveness, only within the restoration of human community as a resource for experienced forgiveness and as a source of ethical counsel, only as it grows from a faith which relates to the meaning of God in the person of Christ. Now if by Kant's statement we mean, "I can only ask radical discipleship of myself if I would wish it for everyone," it makes sense. But the question as usually phrased means rather,

"What would happen if everyone were a conscientious objector while most men were still not Christian disciples?" This is an eventuality which we have no reason to "fear," for it won't happen. It is most unrealistic to think that such calculation would ever be the basis for making our decisions. We must make our decisions on the assumption that most of the world is not going this way, for it does not share our faith. Only then will Christian moral thinking be realistic.

Not only do most people not believe; not only are they not asking us for ethical guidance; but we must make our peace with the fact that this will continue in our age to be the norm. I say "norm" not in the sense of desirability or finality: but we shall not be surprised when the stream of history continues to take another course than the one we propose.

Here lies one of the major debates within the Christian pacifist camp. We have all read the interpretations of what happened as civil rights concern moved beyond the professional core of Christian pacifists to a larger group of people. Almost unconsciously but almost unavoidably, "The Movement" seemed to be making to millions of black people the promise of a new order that no one would be able to deliver; and then the question became acute whether nonviolence is able to produce what it promises, when what it promises is such a solution to society's problems as has never been produced before. If nonviolence cannot "deliver" is violence then justified?

New Testament moral thought begins by facing the fact that we live in a world which most of the time does not listen to all that Christians have to say and some of the time will listen to nothing. Recognition of this minority posture calls not for social cynicism or for withdrawal, but for a profound intellectual reorientation. Going far beyond the mere statistical awareness that not as many people will show up on Sunday morning as used to, this reorientation will move on to the recognition that probably many of those who do attend are not yet committed to orienting their lives around a profound conviction that Jesus Christ is Lord. Continuing to give them practical counsel about how to live just a little better does little ultimate good either to them or to the world.

Professor James Smiley in his *The Christian Church and National Ethos* [4] details embarrassingly the extent to which America has become for its citizens a substitute church. It is from the nation and not the church that man expects salvation in history. It is not the church but the Federal Bureau of Investigation which people are willing to trust to investigate one another's moral character and to decide who is and is not in the community. Now if our hope is that of the American religion, it will be appropriate for our churches to strengthen the moral conviction of our civilization by having nothing to say but "God bless America." Similarly if our hope were that of Marxism, then we would believe that it is through our party's taking over the reins of society that the meaning of history will find its fulfillment. Then our hope for the world would appropriately include the need to rule the world and make every kind of compromise, concession and strategic zigzag that is needed for the party to achieve this end.

The Christian community is the only community whose

social hope is that we need not rule because Christ is Lord.[5] Such hope then goes on into the substance of social ethics to affirm that because it is from the cross that He reigned, because it is "the Lamb what was slain that is worthy to receive power," therefore our faithfulness and the triumph of God in human history are not linked by the mode of direct cause and effect. We do not sight down the line of our faithfulness to His triumph. We do not say that if we behave thus and so the mechanism of society will bring about this and that effect, and the result will be this desirable development or the containing of that particular evil. There is not that kind of mechanically imaged relationship between our obedience and God's fulfillment. [6] Because therefore our hope is in Christ, the prophetic originality which the church must represent in the world is not simply that she has a more sacred cause for the sake of which she can worthily push people around. It is rather that she has a cause which dispenses her — enjoins her — from pushing people around in unworthy ways. The "otherness of the church," toward the discovery of which Christians in our age are moving on several paths, is therefore the test of the clarity of her commitment to a servant Lord.

It was such a discovery that a small circle of Christians made under Adolf Hitler, even though their theological education had trained them to think of the church as the church of only the German nation. It is such an awareness to which worldwide Christendom is being forced by the recognition that Christians in India, in Indonesia, in China, or Japan cannot guide their contribution to their society by the assumption that its survival or its moral character will depend immediately on how effectively they are able to bend or to bless the structures of their society. It is this kind of "disestablishment," not of buildings or bishoprics but of the soul of the church, which is the sole hope of a renewed relevance, whether we be speaking to civil rights or civil marriage, to automation or to war.

We began by noting the paradox of the imperative, "be what you are." Since Constantine, this "something else" that the church has been trying to be instead of "the church," instead of the beginning of a new kind of human relations, has been to be the soul of the existing society. The church has felt she needed to provide religious resources for the morality of Everyman, and it was largely the accommodations necessary to meet that standard which she found legitimized war and violence. It was assumed that if Christians did not take management responsibility for society, there was no one else who could do it and the world would fall apart.

Now we are in an age which often calls itself post-Christian. Christians and the churches recognize that they are not fully in charge. In many places they are not even in the majority. Christians cannot do everything that needs to be done, nor should they need to. The survival of our society is not dependent upon its being controlled by Christians and the effectiveness of government is not dependent upon the willingness of Christians to make all kinds of compromises in order to be able to fill all the necessary offices. They must therefore judge what they do and what they leave to others by the standards of what is most specific, what is most clearly in the line of their primary mission.

Let it be remembered that the failure of the Constantinian vision to produce a reliably Christianized world is not the result of its having been criticized by the radicals or undermined by the sectarians. Constantine and the leaders of his kind of church had control, after all; that was the point of their ethical approach. If then this strategy of being the church identified with the political structure could ever work, if the commitment to be the soul of the total society seeking to save the whole society by baptizing all its infants and counseling its statesmen was ever a viable vision, and could work, it has been given a good try! The end of the Constantinian age comes not because the sectarians argued against it, but because of the contradictions within its own self-assertion. It is not an approach which has not been given a chance but one which, given centuries to work with, has defeated itself. [7]

This recognition that the caretaker function of the church in society will no longer work and is not needed does not in itself provide an argument for pacifism, although it does undermine the reasons which originally led to pacifism's being rejected. For the pre-Constantinian church, which was only a church, idolatry and militarism had coincided; being the minority church, rejecting idolatry, and rejecting militarism were all of a piece. What changed in the fourth century was not a new ethical insight but rather the phenomenon of a Caesar, and a culture, claiming to be Christian. Through the breakdown of Christendom, Christians find themselves again in the position of a voluntary minority. For our grasp of the mission of the church, it may now be more possible to admit to the relevance of the testimony of the pre-Constantinian church, predominantly pacifist from New Testament times until after the age of Tertullian. In that age the logic of thinking from a minority stance, in which saving society is not a conceivable imperative, was clear. The Christians' abhorrence of the idolatrous character of the Roman government and the nonresistant ethic of Jesus combined without question to support that early Christian pacifism.

What changed between the third and the fifth centuries was not the teaching of Jesus but the loss of the awareness of minority status, transformed into an attitude of "establishment." If it was this that helped let the church cease to be the church, then the breakdown of the establishment status of Christianity, while not in any way guaranteeing a renewal of her status as church, might at least open the door to such a renewal. If it was this that helped make the church cease to be pacifist, then the waning of the Constantinian age opens the door to that agenda too. If the novelty of that phenomenon was what brought the ethic of the Roman state into the church, its withering-away at least reopens the question of the status of that ethic in Christian thought.

This much attention has been given to the psychological disestablishment of the church and its implications for ethics because it seems to be at this point that Western Christendom has been most unfaithful in the past and stands today to gain most by saying yes to the shaking of her foundations. But there are other dimensions of being the church which are up for renewal as well in our age and which relate as well to the renunciation of war.

One fruition of the modern missionary movement was that it reminded people "back home" in Christian Europe that most of the world was not Christian. Just as important was that it dramatized the unity of the globe. It is as much the missionary movement as the commercial and political imperialisms of the same age which created for us today the possibility of seeing our one world as a cultural family. *Christian unity is the true internationalism,* for it posits and proclaims a unification of mankind whose basis is not some as yet unachieved restructuring of political sovereignties but an already achieved transformation of vision and community. That all mankind is one cannot be demonstrated empirically nor can it be brought about by political engineering. That all mankind is one must first be affirmed as a theological proclamation. Only then is the engineering and structuring which are needed to reflect it ever conceivable. It could just as well be said that *Christian internationalism is the true unity* which the servant church must let be restored. The original meaning of the word "ecumenical" had to do with a geographical wholeness. Recent decades have brought into more prominence a secondary meaning having to do with divisions among churches on the ground of faith or order, doctrine or sacrament or church structure. As significant as this latter kind of division may be, it is still the dividedness along national lines which has made Christians ready to kill each other: Lutherans kill Lutherans, and Catholics, Catholics. There is a not fully explicable skewing of vision involved when massive

130

institutions seek to reunify the structures and the creeds of churches. Especially within the Western nations such forms proliferate, making not only no progress but, in fact, very little effort toward the development of structures of visible unity which can reach across national boundaries, most importantly, those of nations at war.

Footnotes

1. Doubleday, 1959.
2. See below the discussion of "other lights," pp. 138 ff.
3. My understanding of the unique significance and normativeness of the life of Jesus (rather than all human life) is the theme of my *Politics of Jesus* study, to be published in the fall of 1972 by Eerdmans.
4. In *Biblical Realism Challenges the Nation, Paul Peachey,* ed., Fellowship Publications, 1963, pp. 33 ff.; also printed as a pamphlet by the Church Peace Mission, 1963, and in *Theology Today,* October, 1963, 313 ff.
5. See above, "If Christ Is Truly Lord," pp. 60-65.
6. Alternatives to this mechanical model of the efficacy of ethics are discussed below, pp. 159 ff.
7. J. H. Yoder, "The Otherness of the Church," *The Drew Gateway,* Spring 1960, Vol. XXX, No. 3, and *Mennonite Quarterly Review,* October, 1961.

II. CHRIST THE LIGHT
OF THE WORLD°

This phrase, the general theme of the Third Assembly of the World Council of Churches at New Delhi in 1961, brought with it a very solid freight of precise meaning.

This was the first General Assembly held outside the Western, once "Christian" world; it met in a nation where men of many faiths seek to understand themselves in the glow of many different lights. The imagery of "light" is understandable in any culture (as other phrases such as "high priest" or "Son of God" might not so easily be); the quality of missionary witness which was thereby represented in New Delhi was not a mere happenstance slogan or "theme." The choice of such a phrase in such a place was a confession, a proclamation.

This concentration upon the claims of Jesus Christ represents a long-term special emphasis in the history of the World Council. The original statement of the

°Rewritten from a lecture presented to the Episcopal Pacifist Fellowship at Seabury House, Greenwich, Connecticut, in August 1964.

"basis of membership" in the Council did not refer explicitly to the Bible or to the Trinity, nor to any ancient doctrines, but it did make essential a confession of Jesus Christ. Dr. Willem A. Visser 't Hooft, provisional secretary of the World Council of Churches then in process of formation, when invited to characterize the original theological developments of the wartime period in Europe, responded with a series of lectures on *The Kingship of Christ.* [1] Following a long period of mutually getting acquainted with one another, the *Faith and Order* series of conferences decided at Lund in 1952 that instead of seeking further to negotiate among fixed traditional positions, it should henceforth proceed, even in the area of church confessions and constitutions, to try to begin afresh with Christ. [2]

But the figure of Christ is crucial not only in the context of unity, as a more promising basis of common confession than the comparison of traditional creeds would be, and not only for mission, as one whose human ministry is explicable and can be communicated to man in every culture. Beyond this, the appeal to Christ represents a particular type of confession of truth, a criterion whereby to evaluate faithfulness (and unfaithfulness) within the Christian community.

This most significant impact of the appeal to Christ was therefore first of all that of a criterion for judgment within the "Christian" part of the world. This development was rooted in the impact of Karl Barth, renewing all the theological disciplines by concentration upon the truth claim of Christ. Here too was rooted theologically the spiritual resistance of European churches to Hitler, theme of the book just referred to.

133

Dr. Visser 't Hooft's story of the rediscovery of testimony to the Kingship of Christ is a resounding truth claim within Christendom. It centers upon the Confessing Church as it resisted the designs of the Hitler government. This resistance, feeble but real, centered in the confession of the authority of Jesus over against fixed doctrinal statements or evolving church structures. [3] The threat to Christians in Germany was a conformist movement, the "German Christians," who had taken to an extreme conclusion the traditional Lutheran confession that there is revelation in the orders of creation and in the course of history. They pushed this to the point of the claim that "if God has given us a Hitler, it must be that a Hitler is what we should have." Over against this temptation arose the appeal of the Confessing Church to the normativeness of Christ, echoing the language of the reformation creeds but relating them to a new set of issues, which gave to the resistance of the churches its modest but real character and effectiveness.

The issue to which we are led is one which is technically and traditionally known in the churches as "natural theology": the claim that there is somehow a given body of truth, whose givenness is self-evident to reasonable man, which gives us guidance of a kind and content different from what we might learn from Jesus. Now it happens that it is "truths" of this kind which have to be appealed to in favor of war: the givenness of the nation, the "reasonableness" of the arbitrage of superior power, the "realism" of the criteria of effectiveness and political responsibility, the inacceptability of other alternatives; these are all self-evident truths whose claim is of the "natural" type.

This background comment may have prepared us to make the outright statement of our claim: the issue of war is a crucial and a most typical touchstone. Perhaps it is the most crucial test point for our age, the point where we are asked whether it is ultimately Jesus or some other authority whom we confess as "the light of the world." We have just noted that the claims that need to be made to support an ethical acceptance of war are of the "natural" kind; but this does not lead us to the acceptance of a clear polarity between Christ and "other lights" unless we are clear in what sense Christ as "Light" would point us in another direction. Thus it is most significant that concurrently with the unveiling of the revelation claim of the German Christian movement there was also development of a new way of reading the record of the social humanity of Jesus.

One of the major developments in biblical theology in the past generation has been a new awareness of the whole social humanity of Jesus. Previously, liberal and orthodox theologies alike assumed that the relevance of Jesus to ethics was that of a teacher of morality. One could debate only the specific meaning of His teaching: its scope, how the Sermon on the Mount was meant to be taken, and other issues revolving around the didactic sections of His teaching. His cross or His public career was assumed to have no meaning for morals.

Now it is much more widely recognized that Messianity was for Jesus and for His disciples a political claim, and that His human career was politically relevant. This undercuts not only the idea that He is only a teacher but, in addition, the opposite idea, also widely accepted, that His teaching was ethically irrelevant because He was a rustic not involved in problems of social structure. Or because He was an apocalyptic who thought the world would soon end and therefore had no perspective for social concern. [4] Jesus must therefore be seen not just as a teacher, nor just as an actor on the social scene but in the unity of His teaching and His person. His life is a life according to the Sermon on the Mount; the cross is the meaning of His moral teaching.

It then follows that *the humanity of Jesus is a revelation of the purpose of God for a man who wills to do His will.*

The concept of Incarnation, God's assuming manhood, has often made us direct our thought to metaphysics; asking how it can be that the human nature and the divine nature can be present together in one person. Whether this substantial miracle be joyously affirmed, as in the Athanasian tradition or found unthinkable as for John A. T. Robinson, it seems agreed by all that metaphysics is the question. But when, in the New Testament, we find the affirmation of the unity of Jesus with the Father, this is not discussed in terms of substance, but of will and deed. It is visible in Jesus' perfect *obedience* to the *will* of the Father. It is evident in Jesus that God takes the side of the poor. It is evident in Jesus that when God comes to be King He rejects the sword and the throne, taking up instead the whip of cords and the cross. The gospel is that God does this for His enemies. Then if this is what God

136

reveals Himself to be doing, this is by the same token a revealed moral imperative for those who would belong to and obey Him.

This deepening of the resources for ethics to be found in the person of Jesus was a very needed corrective to some of the temptations of much recent pacifist tradition. A major handicap of an earlier pacifism was its concentration upon the teachings of Jesus in abstraction from His life and from the manner of His death. This concentration was not in itself wrong, but could easily be misunderstood or become superficial. It could seem that pacifists who were concerned to do what Jesus said were thereby unrealistic about the possibilities really available within history for human obedience and achievement, [5] or that they were puritanical in the nearly superhuman demands they would make on the capacity of men to be unselfish and accept suffering, or that they were monastic in the concern for moral innocence and willingness to withdraw from the scene of conflict, or that they were linguistically or semantically naive about how it is possible to interpret precisely the full meaning for all times of a written command.

All these pitfalls are real, and to concentrate upon the words of the command does not protect against them. A fuller feel for the revelatory authority of incarnation is a far-reaching corrective at these points. In the life and death of Jesus we find a reality and the possibility of all that the teachings say. It is possible to live that way *if* you are also willing to die that way.

In the personal case of Jesus it is made clear that He rejects not only unjust violence but also the use of violence in the most righteous cause. It is no longer possible to misinterpret His teaching as simply a call to vigilance or to sensitivity in excluding the *improper* use of violence; what Jesus was really tempted by was the *proper* use of violence. It was concerning the use of the sword *in legitimate defense* that Jesus said that they who take it will die by it!

So we learn from the rooting of pacifism in the person of Jesus that the traditional tension between law and love or between the ideal and possible is artificial.

The result of this total development has been an end to efforts to find justification for war in the New Testament — in the failure of Jesus to tell a centurion to become a conscientious objector, in the silence of John the Baptist about the immorality of the profession of the soldiers who came to him for baptism, in the cleansing of the temple. Increasingly, sober theological criticism of pacifism renounces argument on that level and begins with the assumption of a nonresistant Jesus. [6] This recognition then lays the foundation for a more clear awareness than had obtained in the early theological tradition, that other standards of ethics must be appealed to over against His teaching, if war is to be justified at all. Thus, as was the case in the German Church struggle, behind an issue of political ethics there looms an issue of theological authority.

We can perhaps best illuminate this phenomenon of "other lights" by brief reference to the two most current forms it takes in the debate about war.

The ways this pattern of thought is encountered most clearly today are the traditional doctrine of the "just war," and the contemporary argument of Reinhold

Niebuhr and his disciples on political "responsibility." Quite different in the details of structure, these two patterns of thought nonetheless have in common one particular assumption.

The doctrine of the "just war" must be dealt with far more respectfully than most pacifists have been willing to do. It takes seriously, as the other available thought patterns do not, that there can be an ethical judgment upon the use of violence in the name of the state. Most Christians, after all, do not make this assumption. They more often sympathize with the Maccabean assumption that the violence of the state is itself sanctified by religious dimensions, or with the Machiavellian view that the state is a law unto itself. Wherever any new opening for the moral criticism of the use of violence arises, it is in some way a use of the just war logic, and should be welcomed as at least an opening for possible moral judgment.

Our purpose here is not to analyze the just war theory itself, [7] but simply to take note of the fact that it makes some specific assumptions which in effect claim revelatory authority, i.e., which claim that they ought to be accepted as expressive of the meaning of the will of God.

The "just war" theory grounds its justification of violence in a network of carefully defined, logically appropriate criteria to determine the particular case in which a particular type of violence will be legitimate; the accent of Reinhold Niebuhr is rather upon the imperative of commitment to the use of power for the sake of justice, with less precision (and less conviction that prior logical precision matters) in the definition of particular legitimate cases. But both approaches have in common the fundamental axiom that it is the obligation of the Christian to direct the course of history so that it attains the goals he chooses, in more traditional words, "to be lord" over other men and over the social process.

Now in particular cases we could test this sense of obligation to direct history by asking whether I am a good enough person to have the right to claim for myself such an imperative. Or we could ask whether I am wise enough to know in which direction history ought to move. Or whether I am strong enough to make it move in the way I think it should. On all of these dimensions, the thought of Reinhold Niebuhr has been very sobering. But the more fundamental point at which to face the question is to recognize that the imperative itself "Thou shalt make history come out right," is so deeply founded in our culture that we cannot even perceive that it might be in need of verification.

We have just referred to "that other light" in the particular form of the theory of the just war because it is the most thoroughly worked out body of tradition on the subject, and in the person of Reinhold Niebuhr, who is responsible for the most powerful and creative re-statement of it in contemporary language. It can, however, be said in a host of other ways as well.

There is the language of the "orders of creation," widely trusted in Protestant social thought. Here it is said that because God created a world in which there is authority, whose bearers justify their violence by various moral claims, therefore we must take it on His *creative* authority that He wants us to operate that way. This again is an affirmation which could be tested logically, since the only place we have creation within our view is in a fallen form. But that again is an internal criticism. The positive affirmation is that creation is a channel of revelation whereby we receive an imperative different from that of the work and the words of Jesus Christ. The most articulate formulation of this position in recent Protestant thought has been in the writing of H. Richard Niebuhr, who distinguishes between an ethic of the Son and an ethic of the Father, with God the Father seen as representing the revelatory quality of the created order. [8]

Still another way of defining that "other light" is the claim to immediate revelations by the Holy Spirit. From Montanus in the second century to the "situation ethics" of the mid-1960s, it has been held that if we were to do away with the definite prescriptions of past authority, there would be a clear present authority speaking in our midst, which would give us instructions different from those of the past authority. Once again we would have numerous internal critiques of the "situational" approach. Is everything I think in the situation right? Is there still some meaningful distinction between right and wrong? Can I credit my every idea to the Holy Spirit or are there other spirits too? But again, let us be content to note simply, formally, that this is another way of finding instructions which differ from those of Jesus. Next to the realm of sexual behavior, it is the realm of killing from which the popular writers on "morality in the situation" draw their most striking anecdotes.

In addition to these strands is the attempt to develop an ethic of "self-fulfillment" or a claim of priority for "love," a love whose content is different from that of Jesus' example. What concerns us here is not the differences of these several approaches, which are significant, but what they do that is always the same. All of them make or presuppose a case for placing our faith in some other channel of ethical insight and some other way of behaving, than that which is offered us through Jesus as attested by the New Testament. All these approaches thereby justify my trusting myself to have the wisdom to know, for example, when I may properly sacrifice the life of my neighbor to the righteousness of the cause which I represent. All of them thus find in this other *channel* of ethical insight also another *substance* of ethical instruction. Whereas Jesus instructed His disciples to return good for evil, this other light demands or permits returning a certain amount of evil. While Jesus told His disciples that they should expect to be persecuted, this other light indicates that in some grounds under some circumstances we should cause others to suffer. The one perspective which it is impossible for these approaches to deal with openly is the possibility (which is more than a mere possibility in the biblical witness) that the basic problem of man might not be that there are bad guys out there. It might be that what is most wrong with me and the world is my own will to power and my own calling upon God to legitimate my self-assertion. Not only is it not recognized that the will to power might be the basic trouble of man; it is in fact precisely my will to power, which is, it is claimed, sanctified and authorized by that "other light."

What we have to do with here is then not simply a confusion which makes the gospel message somewhat less categorical or somewhat more humble. It is not a further dimension which makes it somewhat less possible than naive people had thought to "apply directly" Christian insights to social problems. What we have to do with here is fundamentally nothing other than a competitive revelation claim. If I say it is my duty to make history come out right, appealing to the concept of "creation" or of "love driving me to take political responsibility" or to the call of "the situation," in all of these cases I am setting up over against Jesus another imperative and another source of imperatives. It is not simply a supplementary kind of knowledge that speaks to a gap in the teaching of Jesus; it is a contradiction of something He spoke to clearly and centrally. "In the world, kings lord it over their subjects; and those in authority are called their country's 'Benefactors.' Not so with you" (Lk. 22:25, 26).

The concept of revelation is not a clear nor a popular one in the 1970s. Yet whether the recognition be popular or not, every value claim which commends itself to the loyalty of Christians will affirm in some way or other a transcendent authority for what it calls men to do. We need not in this context have a definition of the sense in which Jesus is "revelation" that will satisfy modern philosophy. All that we need for present purposes is to observe, functionally, that the imperative to make history come out right is being given, by those who will weigh it over against the imperatives of Jesus, a normative authority equal to or practically greater than that which they will accord to Him. The very sense of self-evidence which permits the advocates of those "other lights" not to feel any need to justify the truth claims they make is itself all the evidence we need that it has for them that kind of irrational authoritative quality which is traditionally called "revelation."

As it would be worthwhile to demonstrate at greater length, the total body of doctrine of the just war is a kind of begging of the question. It is assumed that a great number of other moral values are solidly known and accepted, so that they can provide a perspective from which to evaluate a given war or the use of a given kind of weapon. It is said, for instance, that war need be waged only by a legitimate authority; but where do we get the definition of legitimacy for political authority? It is said that only such weapons may be used which respect the nature of man as a rational and moral being; but who is to define just what that nature is and what means of warfare respect it? The evil which is sure to be brought about by war must not be greater than the evil which it seeks to prevent, but how are we to measure the weight of one evil against another? A just war can only be waged when there is a clear offense; but what is an offense? In a host of ways, the total heritage of just war thought turns out to be a majestic construction whereby a case is made, on the grounds of the self-evident values which seem to need no definition, for setting aside the examples and instruction of Jesus with regard to how to treat the enemy. In order thus to function, the other values, as well as the logic whereby they operate in the given case, must have a kind of authority for which the best word is "revelatory." Otherwise they could not be weighed against Jesus.

Once we have ascertained that we have to do with a revelation claim, we are almost at the end of our argument. It is possible to explain quite clearly the claim which Jesus made upon the obedience of His disciples to do the will of His Father as He understood it. If someone claims to be a Christian and yet commits himself to other revelatory authorities, then it is, by definition, impossible to debate theologically that option, since it is ultimately the choice of another "light" or another god. This is especially so if they authorize him to turn away from specific implications of following Jesus and choose actions which are less costly or more profitable to one's self or to the extended self of one's own society. I could try to argue that other gods are less worthy of obedience than the one whom Christians call "the Father of our Lord Jesus Christ," or I could argue that it has pleased this One Only God to reveal Himself through the life and ministry and teaching of Jesus Christ as through no other medium; I could even try to argue that people who follow other gods do not turn out to be happy. But all such argument would be beside the point once we have ascertained that the basic issue is whether to set up beside the Jesus of the canon and the creeds some other specific sources and contents of ethical obligation.

Since we are discussing this in an ecumenical context it can further be noted that the appeal to Christ alone, though it was favored as the "style" in the World Council from 1948 to 1961, [9] was discovered also to be

145

the most genuinely ecumenical posture. If I say I am committed to the authority of Jesus *plus* a particular church or of Jesus *plus* common sense or of Jesus *plus* my own best insights, or of Jesus *plus* a particular creedal heritage, that very addition of something extra is structurally sectarian. It makes it impossible for me to converse with those who have a different "plus" or who claim to have no "plus" — and thereby refuse to avow their own historicity. If on the other hand one claims rigorously that the only normative point of orientation can and must be the Jesus of the New Testament witness, then there is no one in the ecumenical conversation whom this excludes, except those who might choose to exclude themselves by their commitment to a specific hierarchy or a special doctrine.

For the Christian pacifist to appeal to Jesus alone is to strengthen his case in conversation with other Christians as over against less worthy kinds of argumentation to which he is often drawn. For the non-pacifist to insist that we must be committed to Jesus plus social responsibility, or Jesus plus the defense of Western liberty, or Jesus plus "the revolution," is to create a new sectarianism which by its commitment to a second value standard renders itself unable to converse further.

Footnotes

1. Willem A. Visser 't Hooft, *The Kingship of Christ,* New York, 1948.

2. Oliver Tomkins, ed., *The Third World Conference on Faith and Order,* SCM, 1953, pp. 15-20.

3. Arthur C. Cochrane, *The Churches' Confession Under Hitler,* Westminster, 1962, especially p. 256: "We reject the false doctrine, as though there were areas of our life in which we would not belong to Jesus Christ, but to other lords."

4. Characterized more fully in my *Politics of Jesus*.

5. Reinhold Niebuhr's simplest negation was always: pacifism considers love to be a simple possibility. Concerning the shortcomings of earlier pacifist positions, compare our pamphlet *Nevertheless: The Varieties of Religious Pacifism*, Herald Press, Scottdale, Pa. 1972.

6. This is the enormous progress which Reinhold Niebuhr, already in *An Interpretation of Christian Ethics*, Harper and Brothers, 1935, makes over more traditional Protestant thought. See pp. 37 ff.

7. Cf. the recent restatement of Ralph Potter, *War and Moral Discourse*, John Knox Press, 1969.

8. H. Richard Niebuhr's "trinitarian" approach is referred to in "Christ and Culture," pp. 81, 114, 131; but spelled out more fully in "The Doctrine of the Trinity and the Unity of the Church," *Theology Today*, October, 1946.

9. 1961 may be said to mark the beginning of a tapering-off of the Christological concentration of World Council thought. Attention began to turn to the "Cosmic Christ" or to "God at work in history" or to "Participation in nation-building"; — concerns for which (it was assumed by many) a specifically Christian stance would be unduly narrow.

Unfortunately this position is not that which was taken by the mainstream of Christian churches for the past 2000 years. Whether Catholic or Protestant, churches generally identified themselves with the power structures of their respective societies instead of seeing their duty as that of calling these powers to modesty and resisting their recurrent rebellion.

When the cultural unity of Christendom began to disintegrate, it was not because churches had seen clearly the path of biblical fidelity. It happened rather because the unity upon which the church had been leaning began to fall apart of its own weight in the century of the "wars of religion" which ended in 1648. It was really only logically possible to think of church and society as a unity, the Holy Roman Church and the Holy Roman Empire, when each of these bodies had worldwide dimensions. Although it was never literally the case, it was at least possible for the Roman Church and the Roman Empire to claim world dimensions. But since 1648 the separated churches were obliged to accept identification with separated specific nation states. This is no longer the unity of the whole church with the whole empire but the unity of a particular provincial or national church with the local government (later we can see a fractioning movement going on even within a given society). Perhaps we should identify this situation as "neo-Constantinianism." It is a new phase of unity or a new kind of unity between church and world. This unity has lost the worldwide character of the epoch of Constantine, yet the fusion of church and society is maintained. We can even say it is tightened, since the wars of religion linked particular churches with particular national governments in a way which had not obtained in the Middle Ages. Now the church is servant, not of mankind at large but, of a particular society; not of the entire society, but of a particular dominating class.

The next logical step in the same direction was to take place in the century of the political revolutions which swept the Western world from 1776 to 1848. Now there begins to be visible a progressive "secularization;" it is now visible that the identification between church and society can no longer be taken for granted; it is society which is withdrawing from the alliance. This can take place, as it has in North America, in that the formal links between church and government are cut away for political or philosophical reasons. But the identification between church and society remains firm in the minds of the people. The United States of America, despite the formal separation, consider themselves a Christian nation, the majority of their citizens consider themselves as members of some church; the army, congress, schools, and even football games have chaplaincy services. In a country like Sweden the secularization process went in another direction. Here the churches continue to enjoy the formal support of government but can no longer count on any important popular support. Different as these two examples are, they have in common nonetheless the fact that they represent the secularization of a Constantian dream. In both cases it is possible that the church can continue to give her blessing to the nation and, that the church

place in Latin America when Christians give their *a priori* approval to the political revolution which they consider imperative and therefore imminent. Such advance approval of an order which does not yet exist, tending to be linked with approval of any means to which people resort which hope to achieve it, we would call "neo-neo-neo-neo-Constantinianism."

Anatomy of the Constantinian Temptation

All of these efforts to defend the cause of the church before the bar of secular analysis have in common the same basic axiom. This is then what is really important; the true meaning of history, the true locus of salvation, is in the cosmos and not in the church. Then what God is really doing He is doing through the framework of society as a whole and not in the Christian community.

Second (for reasons not clearly linked with the former assumption), it is assumed that if we pitch in and help it will be possible as it would not be otherwise to achieve for the world that fullness of salvation which it was already on the way to achieving *by itself*. We will then do well to ally ourselves with the powers which surround us as our way of participating in the creating of a society worthy of men.

It would seem that much distinguishes these views one from another; it would appear that neo-Constantinianism is the enemy and finally the executioner of Constantinianism, and on down the line, so that they have always considered themselves as mortal enemies. As a matter of fact, the most fundamental assumption which they make is the one they hold in common. It

154

is because they want to fight for control of the same terrain that they are enemies; not because one can rise to a higher moral level than the preceding one. All of them together agree to limit the validity of the church, of Jesus Christ, of the New Testament, as sources of moral norms. For them the structure of social development in this world is itself a revelation of what must and should and will take place. In the beginning this "secular revelation" came by way of the power of the emperor of Rome. Today in contemporary secularism this "revelation" is the respect which we have (neo-neo-neo) for the fantastic capacity of our technocratic society to make things work, or else the conviction we have (neo-neo-neo-neo) that everything is so bad that revolution is the only meaningful imperative.

This other "truth," the survival or the prosperity or the development or the restructuring of the national unit, has thus become and remained more decisive than the biblical imperatives. In this sense the church is not seen first of all as a gathering of believers nor as a critic of things as they are. She is rather considered as chaplain to society, providing resources to help people meet specifically spiritual needs. The other assumption which is common to all these kinds of Constantinianism is that it is the business of the church to identify with "our side," with the good guys. It was the churches of the West who supported the action of the United Nations in South Korea. It is the churches of the Socialist countries who take for granted the superior moral value of Marxist secular society. It is the churches of the American Bible Belt which sustain popular

should not be with a simply logical question about pragmatic efficacy. We are supposed to be asking a theological question. Does the gospel give us any indication of how to avoid alliances? Might we not expect to find that the contribution of the Christian church can be more helpful and more efficacious when she maintains her identity distinct from the rebellious powers, even where they seem successful?

It can be argued that this is the lesson of history. The Christian church has been more successful in contributing to the development of society and to the well-being of men precisely when she has avoided alliances with the dominant political or cultural powers. Why should we not expect it to be the same in coming years if the church is going to make a worthy contribution? She must not simply look out into the streets for the evident form of "what is happening in the world" in order to unite herself with this movement in the claim that "it is God who is doing this." Not everything which is happening is the work of God. Instead of asking "What is God doing in the world" should not the church ask herself, "How can we distinguish, in the midst of all the things that are going on in the world, where and how God is at work?" The answer to this question will not be found by reading on the surface of daily history but by the Spirit-guided understanding of the discerning community.

In our age many are profoundly impressed by the needs of oppressed men and tend simply to declare, "revolution is the will of God," feeling that to be a firm statement. But we need to learn to ask a more precise and profound question. "In a world where rev-

158

olutions of many kinds are popular and probable, what is the shape of the revolutionary servanthood to which the disciples of Christ are called?" Whether it be in ancient or future society, this particular calling is to be not master but servants. Thus what we have to discern for the church is not a new way to establish a much more promising alliance with the most constructive powers that we can see at work in society, as much as to discern the shape of the moral independence that is demanded in order to exercise over against these powers the ministry which only the church can exercise, her constant call to sobriety and to respect for human dignity.

Instead of Efficacy

This survey of the successive failures of the varieties of Constantinianism leads us to conclude that our effort to perceive, and to manipulate a casual link between our obedience and the results we hope for must be broken. If we claim to justify the actions we take by the effects they promise, we shall be led to pride in the abuse of power in those cases when it seems that we can reach our goals by the means at our disposal. When we insist on the presence of this link the opposite also happens. We are led to resignation and withdrawal in the cases where we fail. In both cases we are drawn away from the faithfulness of service and singleness of a disciple's mind. We are drawn into the twofold pride of thinking that we, more than others, see things as they really are, and of claiming the duty and the power to move history aright. If our faithful-

wield power as instruments of coercion and pressure, obliging an adversary to yield unconvinced.

The relevance of a transcendent hope includes within it "*wonder.*" Every explanation of the most important social movements, such as the American civil rights movement or the peace movement, has to give serious attention to the dimension of the unexpected and unprogrammed. A full Christian accounting of history must make much of the inexplicable coincidences — the pious call them providential — at certain decisive points. Often brilliant solutions, heroic resistance, reconciling initiatives turn out not to have been the fruit of strategic programming but to have been "given" by the situation in a way which is a surprise, a revelation, "a marvel before our eyes." The most careful strategists see things knocked out of their hands and find solutions which would not have been evident if they had been able to keep on controlling the situation. This is the way it usually goes with the lordship of the Crucified One. His power is not a divine rubber stamp with which He is committed to accredit our best wishes, but rather a treasure in earthen vessels, a force which is made complete in powerlessness.

The relevance of a transcendent ideal is sometimes that of the *unmasking of idols.* There are times when a society is so totally controlled by an ideology that the greatest need is that someone simply identify a point where he can say a clear no in the name of his loyalty to a higher authority. We have no right to say that those who refused to enroll in the racist crusade of Adolf Hitler should first have been obligated practically or morally to propose an alternative social

162

strategy before they had the right to refuse. The imperative of the denunciation of idolatry is not conditioned by our immediate capacity to bring about an alternate world. Many times the nonconformist or the conscientious objector are the ones who discover new and creative social solutions. But the obligation to refuse conformity is independent of the capacity to project such better solutions.

The relevance of a transcendent hope is sometimes that of a *pioneer*. It has often been argued that Anglo-Saxon democracy is traced after the pattern of the congregational meeting of the evangelical churches. It was the church which in other ages invented the work of the school and the hospital, creating institutional models which much later could be generalized and supported by the wider society, by the state. In our age it has been the service agencies of churches which first developed the concept of voluntary service for young people which is now coming to be adopted by universities and governments in various forms of overseas service and Peace Corps. It was the *Christian Committee for Service in Algeria* which first undertook on a very small scale a project of reforestation, beginning a promise to restore to North Africa a part of the agricultural wealth which it possessed before the goats made desert of much of its land. Christians can undertake pilot efforts in education and other types of social service because, differing from public agencies, they can afford the risk of failure.

The relevance of a transcendent hope may sometimes be that of the *spring in the desert*. If, in a desert region, water can be found it is because in some distant

locate the greatest need of man in the wrong place.

The Apostle Paul once wrote, "The weapons of our warfare are not carnal but mighty" (RSV: "not worldly but have divine power"). The implicit set of alternatives is striking. We would have expected him to say "not carnal but spiritual," or "not weak but powerful." There is in this unexpected apposition more than a stylistic slip. The opposite of carnal power is real power; worldly power is intrinsically weak. Those for whom Jesus Christ is the hope of the world will for this reason not measure their contemporary social involvement by its efficacy for tomorrow nor by its success in providing work, or freedom, or food or in building new social structures, but by identifying with the Lord in whom they have placed their trust. This is why it is sure to succeed. The certainty of effect is founded not in our capacity to construct a mechanical model of the connection from here to there, to "sight down the line of our obedience" to His triumph; but rather in the confession itself.

Discerning the Patterns of Providence

Thus far we have been thinking about "history" as the realm of social strategy. We now turn to asking as well whether this "messianic" orientation will have particular implications for history as an intellectual discipline, i.e., for historiography, the recounting of events and the discerning of meanings. Can one gain new light upon the relevance of a Free Church vision of ethics by claiming that it also leads to a new way of interpreting events in the past? Decision in the present is often very much the product of how the past has been recounted to us. If we are then to open up a new future it must be the extension of a rereading of the past. Historiography must be rehabilitated by being taken back from the grasp of the military historians and the chroniclers of battles and dynasties, and informed by other criteria to judge a society's sickness or health.

Instead of reading history as proof of a theory of political science, i.e., the definition *sine qua non* of the state as its monopoly of physical coercion, could we study the story with some openness to the hypothesis that genuine power is always correlated with the consent of the governed or legitimized in some other way? Is there such thing as a "peace church historiography"? There was a time when such a question would have been sufficient occasion for horror-struck reaction from the historians' profession; to read history from any point of view, it was held, is biased and unscientific. One must read from no point of view at all or "objectively." Fortunately the very "objectivity" of the historians allowed this misunderstanding to pass. There is no historiography without a viewpoint; the most honest historiography is not that which claims to be value free but rather that which is open about its prejudices and includes in its methodology a check against their leading it to distort the record.

The following observations, none of them original with the writer, are intended only to make a logical point. Whether the interpretations of the empirical events underlying these analyses are correct is a question I cannot vouch for. The logical appropriateness of

tain. Often the bargains he needed to make to get into the office are the very reasons why, once firmly established there, he is not in the position anymore to help those truly in need — for whose sake he first sought to achieve power. Nor is it to be taken for granted, as popular Marxism has tended to do, that if the "former system" is intolerable, some new strong person will surely be able to solve those same problems more successfully. The new prince is not necessarily more humane than the predecessor; the Marxist theory that the state will wither away once the outside sources of injustice have been eliminated has yet to become practice anywhere. It is not certain that Marxists in government authority are more effectively able to govern in the interest of the population than rulers of other convictions.

Conversely, there are other more useful ways to contribute to the course of society than attempting to "rule." If the history of the Middle Ages is carefully read, we shall increasingly discern that such success as there was in "Christianizing" medieval society was obtained less by the power of the princes than by the quiet ministry of the monastic movements, in rebuilding the community from the bottom. Similarly, what we now call modern civilization was created not by governmental fiat, but by the research of intellectual (and religious) nonconformists, studying the ways of the natural world with the curiosity of the disinterested voluntary searcher. Let us therefore learn to write and to read history as the history of peoples, not of nation states; to evaluate a civilization not by the success of its armies but by how it treated the poor and the foreigner, how it tilled the soil.

Manhood Is Not Brutality

Not only the history books preach a view of man according to which physical and political violence is the ultimate test of the value and of personal merit. It is also the case for popular poetry and literature, all the way from the classical tales of the age of chivalry to the modern morality legends of the Western film, the spy story, and the cover story of the successful businessman in *Time* magazine. What these stories impress deeply upon the soul is not simply the picture of a personage but a view of the universe. They tell us we are in a universe where there are "bad guys" who are utterly beyond redemption. The only satisfactory result of the conflict with them must be that they be banished or crushed. The "bad guy" is not evil because we can know that he has wittingly done evil deeds or expressed malevolent intentions; he is bad by definition, by status, because he belongs to the wrong organization, or to the wrong race.

Then there are the good guys. Goodness, like evil, is not morally based. The good guys lie and kill just like the others; but they are on the right side, they are good because of the cause they represent. This guarantees not only that they have the right to lie and to kill but also that they will always win out in the end.

We have here a picture of the whole moral universe; one which (at least in the United States) has manifestly influenced the national personality and the national style in international affairs, as we can observe in the

171

The only kind of "peace" of which this could with any truth be said was the kind of imperial control which was once called the "Pax Romana." Once there are several nations, instead of one emperor ruling the world, the effect of the armaments race has generally been to precipitate the very wars its advocates (on both sides) claimed they were going to prevent.

The alternative to this self-glorifying identification of "peace" with the predominant power of one's own nation or class is not passive unconcern with the distress of one's fellowman, nor is it utopian expectation about the ability to create a warless world. The alternative is the concentration of Christian attention not on the pragmatic predictability of good results promised by recourse to coercion, but on the creative construction of loving, nonviolent ways to undermine unjust institutions and to build healthy ones.

War Is Not a Way to Save a Culture

The native Indians of North America, when threatened by European invasion, fought back militarily. Even though they had some technical advantages in their knowledge of military methods adapted to the terrain, and even though they were able to play the French and British colonizers off against one another, the Indians of North America were defeated. Their few surviving heirs have been demoralized, their culture has been degraded, their society caved into a rural ghetto.

In contrast to this, the native of what we now call Latin America, facing invaders who were no more gentlemanly, did not fight back in the same way. The

174

Iberian invaders were generally able to sweep over the entire continent, spreading themselves thinner because they met less opposition, even from the highly organized societies of Mexico and Peru. As a result of the inability or unreadiness of the Indians to defend themselves militarily, their population and many of their cultural values have survived to become part of contemporary Central and South American civilization. From the point of view of the European settlers permitting the Indianization of Catholic religion was a dubious form of Christianization; but our question from the Indian side is whether war is a way to preserve one's cultural values. The corruption of Catholicism in Latin America by the absorption of elements of the pagan Indian heritage is a proof of the cultural wisdom of letting the invader enter and "roll over the top" of one's society instead of fighting him to the death.

The fundamental assumption made in all of our society is that, although war is regrettable, almost infinitely so, it would be still worse to see our civilization destroyed. War therefore becomes ultimately necessary for the sake of civilization which, it is held, only war can preserve. This is, however, not a statement about moral logic; it is a prediction about the course of political history. Is it actually the case that war is the best way to preserve a society? Is it the case that national sovereignty is the best way to encourage cultural growth?

As long as the Roman Empire was strong enough to repulse by massive military means the invaders from the north, this military effort not only became increasingly ineffective but it also corrupted and impoverished

be made. The creativity of the "pilot project" or of the critic is more significant for a social change than is the coercive power which generalizes a new idea. Those who are at the "top" of society are occupied largely with the routine tasks of keeping in position and keeping balance in society. The dominant group in any society is the one which provides its judges and lawyers, teachers and prelates — their effort is largely committed to keeping things as they are. This busyness of rulers with routine gives an exceptional leverage to the creative minority, sometimes because it can tip the scales between two power blocs and sometimes because it can pioneer a new idea. In every rapidly changing society a disporportionate share of leadership is carried by cultural, racial, and religious minorities.

What is said here about the cultural strength of the numerical and social minority could just as well be said with regard to *political* strength. The freedom of the Christian, or of the church, from needing to invest his best effort or the effort of the Christian community, in obtaining the capacity to coerce others, and exercising and holding on to this power, is precisely the key to the creativity of the unique Christian mission in society. The rejection of violence appears to be social withdrawal if we assume that violence is the key to all that happens in society. But the logic shifts if we recognize that the number of locks that can be opened with the key of violence is very limited. The renunciation of coercive violence is the prerequisite of a genuinely creative social responsibility and to the exercise of those kinds of social power which are less self-defeating.

By way of conclusion, let us look clearly at what such examples do and do not mean. It might be argued — and is argued by some pacifists — that nonviolent techniques are available or can be found soon which would be successful in defending anything worth defending in any society. Then the feasibility of these techniques and the promise of efficacity is presented as an argument within the prudential frame of reference, i.e., within the acceptance of the idea that the morality of our action is to be measured by its calculable effects in bringing about the possible resulting social situation. What "works" is still what is right: violence never works.

Such an argument, actually basing the rejection of violence on the promise of a better way or proving the relevance of pacifism on the ground of the lessons of history would place in the prudential type of reasoning and the historical type of analysis much greater faith than I can do. I proffer these specimens with a much more modest intent:

1. To support my testimony that the efficacity of violence has not been demonstrated: the prudential frame of ethical reasoning is not conclusive.

2. To demonstrate to the person committed to such a type of reasoning that even within that framework he cannot solidly demonstrate the usability of militarism as a way to save a society.

3. As a testimony that, while disagreeing with a person who reasons thus, I do not make fun of or disrespect his concerns.

4. As a way to testify to a person with a value commitment other than my own that my confessing stance has a relevance to the decisions he makes in the "political" situations used as examples above.

him." The call to those who know Him as Lord and who confess Him as such is not to follow the fallen world in the kind of self-concern which He must overrule, but to follow Him in the self-giving way of love by which all the nations will one day be judged.

When John the seer of the Apocalypse wept at the news that no one could break the seals and open the scroll to reveal the meaning of history, the angelic gospel was that the Lamb that was slain is worthy and able to open and to reveal. To Him blessing and honor and glory and power is given eternally. This is the gospel view of history.

"It is not ourselves that we proclaim; we proclaim Christ Jesus as Lord, and ourselves as your servants, for Jesus' sake." This, and no dreamer's confidence in the inborn goodness of man or the omnipotence of technical organization, enables our patience, our defeat, our confidence.

"We are never abandoned to our fate. . . . Wherever we go we carry death with us in our body, the death that Jesus died, that in this body also life may reveal itself, the life that Jesus lives" (2 Cor. 4:9, 10).

Footnotes

1. "Christ and Power," *The Politics of Jesus*, Chap. IX; cf. H. Berkhof, *Christ and the Powers*, Herald Press, 1962.

2. Hanfred Müller, *Von der Kirche zur Welt*, Leipzig, 1961.

3. Also under Bonhoeffer's influence, Paul van Buren, *The Secular Meaning of the Gospel*, the Macmillan Company, 1963.

4. "The World and the West," Oxford University Press, 1953.

THE AUTHOR

John Howard Yoder is professor of theology and ethics at the Associated Mennonite Biblical Seminaries, Elkhart, Indiana, and is currently serving as president of Goshen Biblical Seminary, one of the member schools of the Association.

Before coming to these positions, the author lived for a time in Europe pursuing both academic and service interests. In 1962 he was awarded the ThD degree from the University of Basel. He participated in the Puidoux series of ecumenical conversations on the church and peace and for many years was a member of the Peace Section of Mennonite Central Committee.

Dr. Yoder is widely known for his vigorous statement of a Free Church theology and is much in demand as a lecturer on peace and ecumenical concerns. His re-